THE EXPERT EDUCATOR

A Reference Manual of Teaching Strategies for Quality Education

ANTHONY S. DALLMANN-JONES, Ph.D.
&
THE BLACK RIVER GROUP

Claudia Bricks, M.S.
Patrick Mealy, M.S.
Rick Osterhaus, M.S.
Steve Smith, Ed.D.

THREE BLUE HERONS PUBLISHING, INC.
303 Gillett Street
Fond du Lac, WI 54935

THREE BLUE HERONS PUBLISHING, INC.
P.O. BOX 463
FOND DU LAC, WISCONSIN 54936-0463
414/921-6991 Fax 414/921-7691

Library of Congress Cataloging in Publication Data
Dallmann-Jones, Anthony S.
THE EXPERT EDUCATOR: A Reference Manual of
Teaching Strategies for Quality Education

Library of Congress # 93-61442
ISBN # 1-881952-23-1

ACKNOWLEDGMENTS

I thank all educators I have had over the years, the good, the bad and the ugly-acting. Each of you taught me something that has brought me to where I am today---writing these acknowledgments after finishing the incredible journey of writing this book. Teachers are the unsung heroes and often the scapegoats and janitors of society's failure to keep its covenant of progressive development with itself. Most of those who cast a critical eye towards education will never know what it is like to stand in front of 25 students at a time every day and demonstrate professional expertise or lack of it.

I thank The Black River Group, of which I am proud to be a member. Never has there been a brighter, more heartfelt, and progressive group of educational think tank futurists! Not only am I appreciative of their writing and editing efforts in preparing the manuscript, but of their vibrant intelligence expressed in our working together. What a fun bunch of educators! Thank you, Claudia Bricks, Patrick Mealy, Rick Osterhaus & Steve Smith!

I thank you Bob Hatch, Larry Rosen, the National Institute of Quality Improvement and Jan and Jim Dallmann for your many ways of giving support. Without people like you, people like me would never be published.

Especially I thank my partner in life, Amy Dallmann-Jones, for her multi-processing of this manuscript from start to finish. I am enamoured of her intelligence, skills, and inner and outer beauty. Her support in thought, work and humor has been outstandingly delightful---and the office snacks have been unbelievable! Thank you for gracing my life, Amy.

...Anthony S. Dallmann-Jones, Ph.D.

TABLE OF CONTENTS

FOREWORD

An Honest Educational Model: Chaos Management

I remember as a child watching the Ed Sullivan Show, a variety hour on Sunday night television. As I recall, about every other year Ed would feature a barrel-chested man in a sequined jacket, a banquet table with a dozen five-foot vertically-mounted dowel rods, and an ominous stack of plates. As the band played upbeat music the man would place a plate on a dowel rod and start it spinning, and then another and another and another. Eventually he would be running frantically back and forth trying to keep the first plate spinning as he attempted to add yet another plate to the procession of precarious china. Towards the climax of the frantic gravity-defying drama he was drenched in apparent anxiety as well as perspiration. At the end, of course, all twelve plates would be spinning to thunderous applause, and the man, with a victorious smile, would take a bow and leave the stage. I remember saying to myself, "If he didn't put all those plates up there in the first place he wouldn't have to work so hard."

A parallel experience is reflected in the many principal-guided tours I have received over the years. Much of school administrators' activities and conversations during my visits have strangely mirrored the activities of the sequined-jacket man. They seem extremely proud of their schools, but particularly concerned about keeping the school quiet, clean, orderly and achieving. Talk about the frantic managing of spinning plates! Over the years I have also noticed that the policy manuals of schools are getting thicker and thicker. My assumption is they are getting thicker because there are more policies, more rules, more guidelines, more regulations, and more standards, in an impossible attempt to keep everyone quiet, clean, orderly and achieving...hedging against the fear of losing that perfect control. This is the fear of *Chaos*, the natural order of things.

Chaos Theory seems extremely pertinent in comprehending the similarities of these two experiences. The man with the plates was trying to make something happen in an organized fashion that was unnatural, and, in order to perpetuate that enterprise, had to exert a great deal of concentration and energy. Administrators have internalized a need to uphold the rules, regulations and behaviors governing a school full of children that must be kept clean, quiet, orderly and achieving---definitely an unnatural act! How often do we create systems that perpetuate a self-fulfilling prophecy justifying the importance of the system...a dynamic *non sequitur.*

If ever there was a time for a paradigm shift in education it is now. It is so past due that it feels silly saying it again. What we see in the hand-wringings of the media, parents, government officials and school personnel is near-conscious acknowledgement of the fact that the horse is already out of the barn. My assessment of what has happened is that the truth is finally *known.* The crime, apathy, and learning, emotional and social disabilities filling our schools tells us clearly that we created a monster of an organization to handle all this only to have the monster turn on us and, at the same time, belie all of the accomplishments that we held up as a measure of our excellence.

A look at Chaos Theory brings us almost instant understanding of what's been going on and what needs to be done in the "restructuring of education." It changes our conception of management to the point that we are less rigid, more understanding, more efficient and effective (and hopefully introduces an epoch of thinner policy manuals!). Those who have approached educational management---both classroom, school-wide, and system wide---based upon the axiomatic beliefs that 1) You can organize away problems; and, 2) Nothing can be gained from disorganization, create The Spinning Plate Syndrome (SPS) requiring constant maintenance and control that becomes a denial-based profession unto itself. We have but to look at our own United States to see examples of how Chaos Theory tells the truth about the way humans actually interrelate and function. Economic figures from the government are displayed by the media as if they encapsulate the whole of the nation's economy with various indices telling us that we are growing or not growing. It is made to appear by these figures that we are in charge of the budgetary factors and that with a little tinkering here and there we can make the figures go up if we really "get determined." No mention is made of shadow economies such as the incredible economic force created by the flow of drug monies in this country, the millions of business dollars that are conveyed under the table, and the monumental figures that are never revealed due to legal and illegal manipulations of taxable income. Yet those monies are real and have major influence to the point that, if they were actually removed from the national cash flow, we would be flirting with economic disaster! We put on our blinders and pretend that 1) these are minor factors, and 2) they are evil factors that should be legally erased as soon as possible. And we make this statement without any apparent awareness of the disastrous results to the economy if those three areas of economic resources vanished.

It is much the same in schools. The Herzberg "informal organization" has more of an impact on how the school runs than the "formal organization" ever thought of having and yet there exists some kind of mutual conspiracy to ignore the fact that emotional crises, cliques, pressure groups, political deals, sabotage of school purposes, and ineffective or superfluous teachings and assessments are not only existant but extremely powerful. Herein lies the need for us to examine Chaos Theory more carefully with its implications for an honest model of educational management both in the classroom, for the school and for the total educational system.

The mindset of school administrators, school boards, parents and state department of education officials is dominated by the physical theories of Archimedes, Galileo, and Newton---the outdated notion that the world is stable and linear, and that you can predict the future if you know the position, characteristics, and velocities of every particle at one moment in time. Newtonian physics is based on the serene assumption that the cosmos is idealistically represented by frictionless pendulums, efficient machines, and endless trajectories. But over half a century ago the founders of quantum mechanics showed us that the world is haunted by randomness and that uncertainty is the rule, not the exception. Even Albert Einstein could not accept this idea and stated that "God does not play dice with the universe!" Well, dice is played with the universe, and with the weather, waterfalls, population fluctuations, oceanic movements, and individual heartbeat patterns and emotional mood-swings. We may be able to control chaos long enough to put a team on the moon (and let's not forget the incredible amount of resources needed for corralling chaos to do this!) but we still can't predict the exact weather, stock markets, trajectories of tumbling dice, or student behavior. Why?

Predictability is played with by the more realistic concepts of Chaos Theory. **Sensitive dependence on initial conditions**, one of its tenets, denotes the precariousness of energy patterns being directed by the most infinitesimal of influences. I once bought a lottery ticket just 10 minutes ahead of an individual who purchased his randomly selected six numbers at the same outlet. His ticket won him $111,000,000...(that's <u>one hundred and eleven million dollars!</u>) My mind has been busy since, fascinated by all the 10-minute events that *could have happened* in his and my life that would have caused us to trade places that evening. In meteorology there is Lorenz's Butterfly Effect that proves that a butterfly flapping its wings over Brazil in February will change the weather in Los Angeles in March. We are everlastingly sentenced to living with chance.

Strange attractors, another Chaos Theory concept, are invisible geometries that draw energy and objects (including people) into unpredictable patterns. Who would have thought Pet Rocks would sell millions? That safety pins would become the symbol of the punk rock movement? That rain would create another Great Lake in the Midwest in 1993? That kids would hang out on a specific street corner, or in certain school hallways, and wear trendy jeans with holes in them? Go figure! One cannot always accurately predict what is going to "draw" energy in certain directions.

Rapid divergence of nearby trajectories, another law of Chaos Theory, states that although things may start out highly correlated, the tendency is to drift apart and become uncorrelated. This is true for relationships between certain motivational strategies and achievement (at first the reward system works well, but sooner or later loses its effectiveness) as well as between humans, i.e., it's natural for us to "shop around."

Proving that inanimate objects are chaotic in their patterns may have been difficult, but it has never been difficult to see this in living organisms, especially humans. Only denial of the truth and fear of losing perfect control has kept us from realizing that we just aren't built that way. It is the **sensitive dependence on initial conditions** in the embryonic stages that creates our individualities right from the beginning. Chaos continues exponentially throughout our lives because of **rapid divergence of nearby trajectories**, separating us from our previous interests and attachments and moving us towards our individually unique **strange attractors.** <u>This</u> is the excitement and beauty of life, and explains why, when we attempt to remove them, that we are left with a dull, irrelevant curriculum and thicker policy manuals. Accepting Chaos Theory's principles will create major positive human- and reality-centered shifts in our school systems. Things will still get accomplished, people will still learn, and education will become a much more intriguing and dynamic system in harmony with the way the world really works.

The typical attempts at educational change consisting of little add-on programs here and little budgetary shifts there will do nothing but further depress us with another chapter in an ongoing chronology of futility. The restructuring of education must begin with the restructuring of our minds...meaning that the necessary paradigm shift must encompass the very minds that conceive it! A reformation is exciting and scary, but if we fail to take the initiative it will occur anyway---only without us. It will appear to happen overnight and it will, according to Chaos Theory, come out of seemingly nowhere. We must learn to notice and utilize spontaneous patterns and "surf the waves of chaos" if we are to make a healthful and productive shift that benefits the children and the society in which they live.

In these rapidly changing times educators must professionally affirm and utilize the prevailing chaotic patterns by being more prepared than ever with an extensive array of internalized tools and skills accessible at a moment's notice. A skilled teacher with a keen mind and a heart for the profession is a sight to behold, and a blessing to the student. It is to this end that *The Expert Educator* is dedicated.

Anthony S. Dallmann-Jones, Ph.D., Director
Institute for Transformational Studies
Fond du Lac, Wisconsin
October, 1993

STRATEGY: An educational method for transforming knowledge into learning.

SUB-STRATEGY: Any medium which enhances the effectiveness of a teaching strategy.

INTRODUCTION

Expert versatility is the central theme of this book. We say this with a certain amount of apology for adding yet another bit of jargon to a field already overburdened with nouveau verbalisms, but we believe it essential in light of the lack of instructional flexibility (i.e., methodological rigidity) so pervasive in classrooms today. Despite the seemingly liberal atmosphere in American society, such movements as accountability, outcome-based education, and back-to-basics are reinforcing education's ever-present conservatism. An unfortunate spin-off of this trend is found in the routinized classroom where flexibility is erroneously viewed as being incompatible with the amplified conservative emphasis of today. This is a serious judgmental error. The concept of "variety" is actually outside the liberal-conservative continuum of educational issues. *Expert versatility* refers to the ability of the instructor to better serve students' subject matter needs, and has nothing to do with undermining current trends or philosophies in education.

All teachers need to vary their teaching strategies in different classroom situations, but most competently utilize only a few, and many only one. This severely limits the teacher's overall effectiveness. When a teacher relies upon a single approach (such as *drill* or *lecture*) as an instructional strategy, student boredom can easily create learning/discipline problems. A beginning psychology student who has studied brainwashing techniques knows the mentally aberrant effects of repetition and boredom. Fantasy, daydreaming, mental-dulling, and even hallucinations are natural outgrowths, and all beyond the individual's control (despite a command to "Pay attention!"). A teacher's lack of expert versatility is indicative of a lack of knowledge of students' needs, interests and individual optimal learning conditions. It is, in effect, a very detrimental form of professional ignorance.

The purpose of this book is to illustrate in a straightforward manner the different types of strategies (teaching methods) and sub-strategies (instructional media, or audio-visual aids) available to teachers attempting to expand their repertory of teaching tools. There are at least five solid reasons for a teacher being proficiently prepared in a wide assortment of strategies/sub-strategies:

1. Different students learn best in different ways at different times;

2. Some subject matter is best served by use of a particular strategy/ sub-strategy or combination thereof;

3. Diverse objectives call for diverse approaches to meet the objectives;

4. The innate abilities of the teacher may determine the effectiveness of some strategies/sub-strategies; and,

5. Environmental factors (money, supplies, facilities, time, etc.) often dictate which strategies/sub-strategies will be most effective.

An Instructional Model

A short and simplistic model of instruction will illustrate the functional relationships of teaching strategies and sub-strategies to the total learning situation.

The instructional decision-making process demands that through observation, conversation, and assessment of/with the students the teacher determines the needs, interests and individual learning styles pertinent to construct a viable learning module or lesson. A well-planned lesson includes objectives, instructional strategies and sub-strategies, and means of evaluating degrees of success in accomplishing objectives. This book is concerned with the total learning module (lesson), but places the heaviest emphasis on strategies and sub-strategies---the body of the lesson. Further description is offered in the Planning for Teaching section of this chapter.

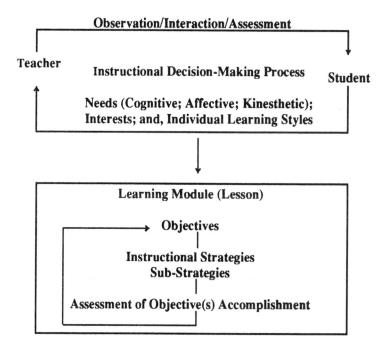

The mastery of instructional strategies is only one dimension of the skills, attitudes and knowledge needed by the competent teacher. For example, no amount of strategies can make up for a lack of content knowledge. The converse is also true. The greater the teacher's knowledge of the subject, the more freedom he or she has to apply a variety of instructional approaches. An expert teacher should also have a basic understanding of philosophies of education, learning theory, learning styles, teambuilding, human development and assessment skills to act as a guide in the proper application of each strategy. The teacher must answer such questions as: What *is* a student to me? What are the student's needs, wants and interests? What is this student's optimal learning style? What does a learner transfer from one experience to another? How do I assess this student accurately? Etc.

Any teaching strategy which is inconsistent with the student's desire for peer acceptance and approval is likely to meet with strong resistance. Even the most careful planning cannot produce beneficial results unless the student personally feels the need for learning. This requires consideration of the associated problems of providing adequately for individual differences. It is a rare student who will not create a disturbance (internally, if not externally) when class expectations are too high or too low for his/her capabilities. Yet, some teachers consistently expect all members of the class to read the same book, do the same problems and perform on the same level by themselves without talking to peers. As a result, these teachers often find their energies devoted to control problems. It is not that the teachers involved prefer a "lock-step" rather than an individualized curriculum; it is simply that they are at a loss as to how to go about creating the more desirable approach. It is hoped that this book will aid in that direction.

Utilization of This Book

Strategies and sub-strategies included herein are defined and described in their "pure form." After practice with a given strategy/sub-strategy has provided confidence in its use in the classroom, it can be combined and blended into new and creative patterns with others. The knowledge, accuracy, and rapidity with which a teacher can apply strategies to a particular learning situation are some of the factors which differentiate the teacher as technician from the teacher as a professional. Both stages are necessary, but one is a rung on the ladder to becoming the other.

The information in *The Expert Educator* is intended for a particular kind of reader: The one who is interested in learning which teaching strategies/sub-strategies to utilize, when they can be used to best advantage, and why they should be used at a given point. This material is not intended to be a recipe book for all the ills of teaching. It is designed to aid and assist teachers in being more selective when choosing a strategy or sub-strategy for a particular educational purpose. It may help to reduce the overuse and possible abuse of the *lecture* method as a standard daily technique for many teachers and place this method in its rightful place as a technique for transmitting information in an autocratic fashion to passive student listeners---a low-level cognitive function. Too often as teachers we tend to use that strategy which gives us a feeling of security. Consequently there is a hesitancy to employ more appropriate methods. Through understanding how different strategies/sub-strategies can best be used, we can encourage ourselves to try new ways to benefit the students.

Most curricular textbooks include some of the teaching strategies found in this publication. However, the efforts here have been directed towards compiling all the existing effective teaching strategies and presenting each in a systematic and concise fashion to aid the reader in determining suitability for a particular lesson. The organization and explanation for each teaching strategy has been uniformly developed and includes the following:

I.   *Definition and Description* briefly defines and/or describes the strategy and occasionally includes clarifying examples. Mention may also be made of other strategies explained in greater detail in a separate section.

II. *Advantages and Special Purposes* includes a list of advantages or special purposes inherent in the strategy.

III.   *Disadvantages or Limitations* lists the disadvantages or limitations to consider prior to selecting a strategy. Disadvantages should not be looke upon as deterrents, but rather as "preventive maintenance" problems to be overcome by practical planning.

IV.   *Guidelines for Maximum Utilization* spells out some ways in which the strategy can be utilized with maximum efficiency.

V.   *Summary* is a concluding statement.

VI.   *Questions to Promote Discussion* provides thought-provoking questions for teachers or future teachers.

The sub-strategy section (Part 2) includes sections I, II, III, and IV above, but not Summary or Questions sections. It is suggested that sub-strategies be selected only after the teaching strategy for the lesson has been decided. This assures a more compatible and effective blend of instructional technique.

TEACHER EXPECTATIONS
AND STUDENT ACHIEVEMENT

Educators can predict with great accuracy student's ability to achieve in school. We look at traits like appearance, attitude, participation, articulation, behavior and social interaction and we draw conclusions as to what that student may possess in abilities and skills. We even create a bell curve and assign grades based on our assessment.

Research conducted in the early 1970's (Kerman, et al.) reveals that teachers also behave discernibly differently toward low achieving students and high achieving students. Teacher interaction with low achieving students is less motivating and less supportive. The bias is not ususaly intentional, but is generally subconscious. Still, the effects are long term and damaging to the child.

The principles of TESA (Teacher Expectations and Student Achievement) are based on recognition of the concept of the looking-glass self. Teacher expectations determine teacher behavior which in turn shapes student behavior and drives student achievement. A teacher with low expectations for a child will reveal behaviors that express that low expectation. The child picks up on the message and responds with behavior that diminishes opportunity for experiencing success in the school.

The Effective Schools Research of Ronald Edmonds (1982) revealed that high expectations for all students will increase the success opportunities for all students. If we believe that inner city minorities can and will learn and our teaching behavior conforms to that belief we increase the odds that learning will take place among those students we have previously perceived as being low achievers. The research of Kerman, Kimball and Martin (1970) adds volumes of evidence to that finding. Where teachers improved interaction patterns with students, notable improvements were made in terms of achievement.

In their research, TESA advocates (Kerman, et al.) found that teachers exhibited a bias in fifteen different interaction patterns with students. That is to say they responded favorably to high achievers in a variety of ways and unfavorably to the low achievers. If teachers were equitable in the interaction patterns listed below, treating high and low achievers alike, low achievers would begin to respond more favorably in class.

An instructional strategy for reaching all learners should take into consideration three categories each including five interactions.

A. RESPONSE OPPORTUNITIES:

1. Equitable Distribution of Response Opportunities

For a variety of reasons, teachers are more likely to call on high achievers when looking for an answer. A correct and rapid answer will keep the pace of the class moving so that we can cover the lesson plan and eventually the book. We believe the high achiever will give a more thought-provoking answer that rewards the teacher's efforts and is intellectually satisfying as well. The teacher may be reluctant to embarrass the low achiever. Eventually a pattern emerges in the classroom and then the school, from room to room, from year to year. High achievers get the questions, low achievers do not. the message to the low achiever is this, "The teacher does not believe that I am able to answer the question." Eventually the child believes that and becomes less able.

What should we do? Provide response opportunities to low achievers as often as to other students in the classroom.

2. Individual Helping

Teachers recognize that all students need help. Low achievers do ask for help and will seek attention. TESA researchers (Kerman, et al.) have found that high achievers and average students are more aggressive in seeking help. They are more frequently assisted by the teacher and spend more time in one on one help situations with the teacher. Again the teacher can easily be drawn to those students who will more than likely absorb the guidance provided and reward the teacher by revealing successful acquisition of the new knowledge.

3. Latency

The wait time that we allow a student between the time that we ask a question and then cut the students off. Again, studies reveal that high achievers receive more time to answer questions than do low achievers. When low achievers fail to respond immediately it is assumed that they don't know, or don't have the skills to answer. It is assumed that a high achiever is in the process of deep thinking and about to emerge with a bright response if given the time to construct the answer. When the high achiever hesitates the teacher will wait. When the low achiever hesitates the teacher will offer someone else, maybe a high a achiever, the question so the student can get it right and the class can move on. Or, the teacher will provide the correct answer.

What should we do? Give all students equal time to respond to a question or task.

New Message: My teacher is giving me time to think.

4. Delving, Rephrasing, Giving Clues

When low achievers are asked questions they frequently get the easiest questions, or the teacher will provide no clues to help them find answers because the teacher assumes it would be a waste of energy and time.

What should we do? Provide additional, follow up information and clues to all students.

New Message: My teacher is giving me the same extra help the "smart kids" get in this classroom.

5. Higher Level Questioning

On Bloom's Taxonomy of Educational Objectives research indicates that teachers are most apt to ask low achievers questions that would only require recall of information. Teachers are more likely to ask other students for the answers that require comprehension, application, analysis, synthesis and evaluation. The more gifted a student is perceived to be the more likely they are to receive higher level questions which require evaluation or synthesis to formulate an answer.

What should we do? Challenge the thinking ability of low achievers as often as other students by requiring more than memorization and recall.

New Message: My teacher insists that I think, that I use my head too.

B. FEEDBACK

1. Affirmation or correction

People of all ages need feedback on how they are doing. Good and Brophy (1971) found that teachers are not only less likely to call on low achievers, but also provide less feedback to them after they have responded. Teachers are more likely to respond to and reinforce high achievers.

What should we do? Give feedback equally to all students.

New Message: I am going to know right away if my work is acceptable or not.

2.   Praise of Learning Performance

High achievers receive praise more often than do low achievers.

What should we do? Praise the learning performance of the low achiever as frequently as the higher achiever.

New Message: My teacher is pleased with my work.

3.   Reasons for Praise

Extended feedback which tells a student why we like their work is rare with any student. When extended feedback is given it is usually to explain what we don't like about their work. All students need more reasons for praise. Flanders (1961) found that we provide low achievers with even fewer reasons for praise than high achievers.

What should we do? Tell low achievers what we like about their work as frequently as we tell high achievers.

New Message: My teacher mirrors positive messages to me.

4.   Listening

A number of inequities exist in listening skills. Teachers tend to listen better to high achievers. Teachers tend to lecture less with high achievers and listen more. Teachers listen more carefully to the questions of high achievers and respond more directly to the satisfaction of those students. Teachers will listen more carefully to the responses of high achievers and seek to shape the right answer out of what they have given.

What should we do? Listen actively to all learners.

New Message: The teacher tunes in to me. The teacher really seems interested in my response.

5. Accepting Feelings

The ability to use the feeling tone of a student is a rare ability. Students may learn more in classrooms where teachers are empathic listeners able to accept the emotions expressed. Teachers who have been taught to suffocate their own feelings may find it impossible to deal with other's feelings. Teachers tend to relate to the feelings of those students to whom they feel closest.

What should we do? Convey to students that emotions are important, that their feelings are accepted and understood. Your emotions are not judged in this classroom.

New Message: My teacher knows how I feel, and I am okay with that.

C. PERSONAL REGARD

1. Proximity

High achieving students tend to be seated in the front row or in the first three seats front to back down the center aisle. They receive as much as 63% of the teacher interaction. (Rist, 1970). Low achieving students are frequently isolated at the back of the classrooms where teachers are less likely to travel. Teachers tend to stand near high achievers.

What should we do? Maintain proximity with all students. Be within an arm's reach of each child as the day proceeds.

New Message: My teacher is close by. My teacher doesn't seem to avoid me, seems to be comfortable near me and I am not threatened.

2. Courtesy

Ray Rist (1972) found that kindergarten students emulated teacher interactions with students. High achievers modeled their relationships with low achievers after the example set by the teacher. High achievers cliqued together and saw themselves as uniquely better than low achievers. Their behavior included lack of respect and courtesy for the low achiever.

What should we do? Use courteous words as frequently with low achievers as with other students.

New Message: My teacher likes and respects me.

3. Personal Interest/Compliments

Teachers are more apt to take time to listen to the personal stories of high achievers. By refusing to listen to low achievers we tell those students that their lives are less significant.

What should we do? Give personal compliments to low achievers as frequently as we do to high achievers. Allow them to relate their personal stories. Express personal interest in their lives as well.

New Message: I am more than just another body in the classroom. I am important to the teacher.

4. Touching

We are concerned here with the inequity that exists between the frequency with which a teacher may touch high achievers versus low achievers. A teacher may choose to not touch students at all, and there are some students who will not allow us to touch them. Where we do use touch to build trust and bonding we must be cognizant of the pattern of our behavior.

What should we do? If we use touch, touch high and low achievers in a friendly and appropriate manner equally.

New Message: My teacher likes me.

5.   Desisting

When a teacher tries to stop a student's misconduct we use the word desist to describe the interaction between the teacher and student. Inequities are found in teachers' desisting interactions. Teacher communication with low achievers is dominating and revolves around conflict. Teacher communication with high achievers tends to be more supportive. Teachers are more apt to be polite when seeking the attention of high achievers who are not on task. Low achievers are more apt to receive criticism, direction, put downs and authority posturing from the teacher.

What should we do? Become as calm in correcting low achiever behavior as we are with high achievers.

New Message: The teacher is upset with my behavior, but not with me as a person.

Advantages of TESA

1.   All students get fair and equal treatment from the teacher.

2.   All students have an opportunity to feel good about themselves.

3.   Opportunities for success for all students exist.

4.   Low achievers find less evidence from the teacher that they are expected to do less.

5.   Teachers enhance the self-esteem of all students allowing them to see themselves as capable and lovable.

Summary

The Pygmalion Effect results when a child receives and believes the subtle and blatant messages from others who have begun to stereotype them as "trouble," "lazy," "slow," "at risk," "special education." What teachers believe about their students shapes that child's behavior. The principle of the looking-glass self is very real. We feed children verbal and nonverbal messages on a daily basis. We are their mirror and the feedback they get when they interact with our mirror feeds their self-concept. If we tell them they are trouble they will prove us right. If we tell them they are lazy they will live up to the image. Teachers need to examine what they believe about children and understand that their interaction patterns with those children feed or starve the children's self worth.

[For more information use the available bibliography at the back of this text, check college offerings for TESA or GESA (Gender Expectations Student Achievement) classes and/or workshops.]

PLANNING FOR TEACHING

This book can improve one's ability to present viable and interesting lessons to students of any age, but selection of a strategy is *not* the primary step. A good plan of action incorporating appropriate strategies is the starting point of organized education, thus insuring a greater probability of success while minimizing learning irrelevancy.

The teacher's plan of action is called a "lesson plan." The lesson plan is to the teacher what the blueprint is to the architect, the script to the director, and the flight plan to the pilot. It is a guide to assist the teacher and pupils in determining the direction of learning. It, like the three analogous examples, is time-consuming if done well.

The Lesson Plan

The lesson plan has three basic components. They include: (1) the objective(s), (2) the body of the lesson, and (3)assessment. (A fourth component is sometimes included and is called "reteaching.") A brief discussion of each of the components is reviewed below to assist you in preparing lesson plans. (A rather extensive treatment of forms of assessment is presented in Part Three).

Objectives

Benjamin Bloom and Robert Mager have repeatedly stressed the value of well-stated objectives in the planning of learning activities. As in planning a trip the first concern is, "Exactly where am I going?" The destination (objective) must be determined before further planning can be effective. Further, the more specific the objective, the easier it is to accomplish it (e.g., tell a New York City cab driver, "Manhattan," when you really want to go to 542 Park Avenue, and see where you wind up!).

In the lesson, what is it that the teacher hopes the pupils will learn? What do the pupils themselves want to learn? How well are they expected to achieve? These and similar questions form the basis of learning objectives. An example of an acceptable mathematics objective might read as follows:

> At the end of this lesson in mathematics, the student will be able to correctly divide a 4-digit number by a 2-digit divisor. Long division procedures will be used, carrying out the answer one place and rounding off to the nearest whole number. The student will correctly work 7 or more of the 10 problems assigned.

It should be clear to the teacher and the students just what is expected in this exercise. Both will know whether the lesson has been successfully carried out and whether any reteaching is necessary. Notice, again, how *specific* the statement of the objective is, and how much more clarity it provides than: "The student will understand long division." Chunking down learning into easily understood pieces may not solve all the teacher's problems, but it certainly will not create any more.

Body of the Lesson

The body of the lesson is the activity portion of the lesson. Having determined the objectives, one must then decide what methods or strategies can best enable accomplishment of those objectives.

Determining which teaching strategy to utilize is the choice of the teacher based upon: (1) knowledge of the learner's needs and/or interests; (2) school and classroom environmental constraints; (3) time and space considerations; (4) subject matter variables; (5) desired collaborative skill involvement; (6) student learning styles; and, (7) capabilities and limitations of the strategies themselves.

The teaching strategy, the ability of the teacher to effectively utilize the strategy, and student ability and interest in the strategy-content combination will eventually determine the success or failure of the lesson.

Sub-strategies (instructional media) are enhancers of strategies. They can either support, amplify, or "decorate" a lesson to make it more attractive and/or magnify its impact. In many cases, they can make the difference between an effective lesson and a lemon. Sub-strategies are detailed in Part Two.

It is suggested again that the teacher become familiar with each strategy and sub-strategy in this book (first by study and then by using each one). This will provide an experiential and more accurate basis for accomplishing this book's goal: An educator who can create a thriving learning environment by surfing the waves of chaos with appropriate on-the-spot strategy/sub-strategy selection to create quality outcomes in the learner.

Assessing/Processing

Measuring accomplishment of learning is still one of the most controversial issues in education, and it may always be. A reason behind this is the depersonalization inherent in most forms of evaluation. For example, I can remember sweating through a course in statistics. Never did I study so hard or pile up so much frustration in one course before or since. Most memorable, however, is receiving the grade in the mail (No, I'm *not* going to tell you what it was!), staring at that little letter, and hearing an old song I heard once run through my head like a repetitively taped message, "Is that *all* there is?" That evaluative designation said nothing of the long hours of study, the many days spent solving long and arduous problems, the incredible amount of formula memorization, and the anxiety-producing test sessions. It did *not* describe how much I had achieved compared with what I knew at the beginning of the term, nor did it describe how well I had done compared to the instructor's course objectives. But, *especially*, it did not portray the emotional obstacle course I had been forced to undergo. I resented it. Utility is found from this experience in that my attitudes concerning the fairness and emotional aspects of assessment have certainly been liberally expanded.

Evaluation does, of course, have other more meaningful forms than test-for-a-grade. A good variation is exemplified by the long division sample objective. A properly written learning objective provides almost automatic evaluation. In the example previously given, if a student correctly completed 7 of the 10 problems, he/she has met the objective and is ready to move up in the division sequence. In other words, a well-written objective includes the evaluation component. Another example:

> The student will be able to diagram and label correctly the chambers of the human heart and illustrate with arrows the flow of blood through all four chambers.

This tells the student what the teacher expects him/her to learn, and, better still, how he/she must *demonstrate* that learning. This type of cognitive learning objective eliminates confusion and guesswork for both student and teacher. Further, it is "fair" in that the student is evaluated solely on the basis of the stated objective, rather than on peripheral learning the teacher feels the student should "probably" have internalized.

What is being discussed here is an alternative to tests as the only evaluative procedure. Ideally, a teacher has students performing demonstrable activities daily in all content areas. Accurate observation of everyday student performance is as valid an evaluative criterion of learning as is test-taking. Esler echoes this in his *Teaching Elementary Science*:

> "We have traditionally been victims of a test-culture, and teachers have shunned all but the test in evaluating progress of pupils. Hopefully, we are now breaking away from this fixation and are recognizing that the satisfactory completion of daily tasks may tell us more about a student than all of the tests he may take."

The *portfolio* method of evaluation that has recently made its appearance in education speaks well to Dr. Esler's point made in 1977. (See more on *portfolios* in Part Three.)

Group Assessment

Instructional feedback for the purpose of improving teaching can be gained by analyzing the achievement of an objective by the total class.

Did a number of students fail to achieve the objective? Were a number of students obviously disinterested or confused during the lesson? Were there students who failed to master any of the objectives? Affirmative answers to these questions should prompt the teacher to review how the lesson was taught:

a) Were the objectives clear and appropriate in relation to the ability of the class?

b) Had the students mastered the requisite skills and knowledge necessary to perform the lesson successfully?

c) Was the teaching methodology appropriate to the subject matter and student learning styles?

d) Was evaluation matched to the stated objectives?

e) Were peer interactions within groups a determinant?

It is establishment of this type of a continual feedback loop that promotes expertise in teaching and productivity in learning.

Summary

Lesson planning is time-consuming but rewarding in that it provides for accountability and quality learning. The teacher and student both profit by having direction without eliminating versatility or flexibility in lesson presentation. Furthermore, the teacher has a viable opportunity to examine his or her own skills in relation to the skills of the students. The outstanding teacher has already learned this lesson well. The beginning teacher and those experienced teachers who have met with difficulty previously should find good lesson planning one means of moving from a mediocre to an exceptional level of performance.

MULTIPLE INTELLIGENCES & LEARNING STYLES

People are unique? No doubt about it. People's unique characteristics are valued equally? Not true. It is fairly well accepted by most enlightened people that each of us is justifiably different and that this is one of the wonderful things that makes life exciting. We do not, however, equally prize those different attributes, nor do we plan for, or even allow for, those inherent differences. It is not unusual for people to be negatively treated specifically because of their inherent differences. This should certainly be an unacceptable condition in that faction of our society dedicated to broadening the knowledge base of our lives: Educators and the schools they live in.

Multiple Intelligences

People are "smart" in different ways. Some cultures value different forms of intelligence more than others, and for specific events admiration for varied forms is evident, such as the ingenious hunter-tracker, a fluid-fingered guitar player, or an intuitively successful gambler. But most of the schools in the world only place a high value on two of the seven basic forms of intelligence, that of *linguistic* and *logical-mathematical*.

In "*Seven Kinds of Smart*" Thomas Armstrong (1992) clearly summarizes Howard Gardner's Multiple Intelligences Theory. The MI context suggests that teachers:
1) Acknowledge the different "ways of knowing" in their students;
2) Affirm those different intelligences;
3) Plan learning activities that support the affirmation;
4) Be willing and capable in utilizing varied teaching strategies that support the learning activities.

This asks a teacher to be informed, affirming, a planner, and strategically versatile.

Multiple Intelligence Theory Implications for T.E.E.
(with permission from and acknowledgement to Thos. Armstrong)

MI Form	Core Components	Instructional Activities
LINGUISTIC	language sensitivity	discussion, lecture, word games, journaling, (reading; writing; listening; talking)
LOGICAL-MATHE-	numeric and logic sensitivity	problem-solving, laboratory, inquiry, Socratic, research, (critical thinking; quantifying; conceptualizing; calculating)
SPATIAL	visual-spatial capacity and manipulation	visuals, art activities, metaphors, synectic, (seeing; drawing; visualizing; colorizing)
KINESTHETIC	movement sensitivity	drama, demonstration, hands-on learning, dance, sports that teach, (Building; touching; dancing; acting it out)
MUSICAL	sensitivity to rhythm, pitch, timbre, and music expressiveness	tapes, musical instruments, (singing; rapping; listening to rhythms)
INTER-PERSONAL	sensitivity to other people and their moods, desires and motivations	cooperative learning, peer tutoring, simulations, (socializing; collaborating; teaching, interacting)
INTRA-PERSONAL	sensitivity to one's own emotional life and strengths and weaknesses and ability to discriminate among them	individualized instruction, independent study, role-playing, value clarification, journaling, (introspecting; choice-making; self-expressiveness)

The MI chart is obviously condensed, but illustrates the many potential flavors of the learning environment when one considers the validity and beauty of human differences. An effective teacher should broaden their depth of expertise in this as well as in the next related area.

Learning Styles

Closely related to the concept of MI is the truth that people learn better in different ways or styles. It is important for the learner to have a teacher aware, affirming and accommodating of this fact. There are many ways of looking at styles of learning and we offer this one as worthy of consideration.

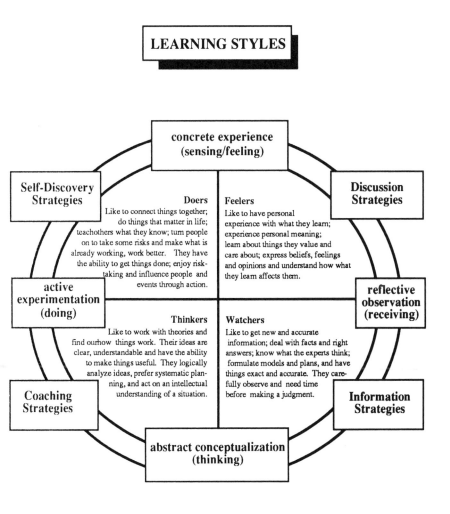

LEARNING STYLES

concrete experience (sensing/feeling)

Self-Discovery Strategies

Discussion Strategies

Doers
Like to connect things together; do things that matter in life; teach others what they know; turn people on to take some risks and make what is already working, work better. They have the ability to get things done; enjoy risk-taking and influence people and events through action.

Feelers
Like to have personal experience with what they learn; experience personal meaning; learn about things they value and care about; express beliefs, feelings and opinions and understand how what they learn affects them.

active experimentation (doing)

reflective observation (receiving)

Thinkers
Like to work with theories and find out how things work. Their ideas are clear, understandable and have the ability to make things useful. They logically analyze ideas, prefer systematic planning, and act on an intellectual understanding of a situation.

Watchers
Like to get new and accurate information; deal with facts and right answers; know what the experts think; formulate models and plans, and have things exact and accurate. They carefully observe and need time before making a judgment.

Coaching Strategies

Information Strategies

abstract conceptualization (thinking)

Learning styles chart explanation

Modes of Experiencing

LOCUS ORIENTATION:
> concrete experience - abstract conceptualization
> This continuum represents the tangible sensing of the world through direct utilization of the five senses of touch, taste, hearing, smelling and vision at one end to the rational ability to conceptualize the world mentally (imagination) at the other end.

ENERGY ORIENTATION:
> active experimentation - reflective observation
> This continuum represents pro-active "doing" at one end and passive receptivity at the other end.

Learning Style Dimensions

FEELERS - (convergence of concrete experiencing and reflective observation continuua) Like to have personal experience with what they learn; enjoy learning about things they value; moved to express their beliefs, emotions, and opinions; tend to understand how what they learn affects them. Feelers are oriented heavily towards a socioemotional reality.
[Strategies that work best: "discussion" strategies]

WATCHERS - (convergence of abstract conceptualization and reflective observation continuua) Like to get new and accurate information; feel comfortable dealing with facts and "right" answers and what the experts think; like to formulate models and plans and have things exact; Like to cardfully observe and need time before making a judgment. The watchers are oriented towards introversion, i.e., focus on internal representations of reality.
[Strategies that work best: "information" strategies]

THINKERS - (convergence of abstract conceptualization and active experimentation continuua) Like to work with theories and discover how things work; their ideas are clear and understandable and have the ability

to make things useful; they logically analyze ideas, prefer systematic planning, and act on an intellectual understanding of a situation. Thinkers are oriented towards isolated exploration of an uncertain reality.
[Strategies that work best: "coaching" strategies]

DOERS - (convergence of active experimentation and concrete experiencing continuua) Like to make connnections and do things that matter in life; enjoy teaching others what they know, inspire others to take risks, and make things better; they have the ability to get things done and enjoy taking risks; they influence others and events through action. Doers are oriented towards extroversion, i.e., focus on external representations of reality.
[Strategies that work best: "self-discovery" strategies]

Humans delightfully defy classification for very long (typical Chaos Theory pattern!) but it is still the expert educator who can be humble enough to discover the learning style patterns into which individual students generally fall, and then match strategies of teaching to each of those styles whenever possible. Notice that this has nothing to do with the content of teaching, but with the delivery system of that content. Matching of teaching strategy to learning strategy can make all the difference in absorption and retention of lesson content. As a famous bartender once said, "It's not how you mix the drink, but how you sit it on the coaster."

Part One

TEACHING STRATEGIES

*Educational methods for transforming
knowledge into learning*

BEHAVIOR MODIFICATION

Definition and Description

Behavior Modification is the term assigned to the application of laboratory-derived principles of learning to behavior problems which may be academic, social or emotional in nature. In practice, Behavior Modification may include such procedures as operant conditioning, contingency management, behavior modeling, role playing, and other planned techniques of attitudinal change.

Behavior Modification may also be known as behavior therapy or behavior management. It has been researched mostly with atypical children; however, the approach offers much for the teacher who desires to use the principles of operant conditioning to decelerate undesirable student behavior and accelerate desirable student behavior in the classroom.

Essentially, certain behaviors are established as desirable for students. Students who exhibit such behaviors, or who move in the direction of the prescribed behaviors, are rewarded in the hope that this will increase the likelihood of the behavior continuing. The reward may be of a verbal nature (such as the teacher saying "good job"), material rewards, or an increase in student privileges.

A program in Behavior Modification is not a panacea for all motivational issues. It is a tool to be used selectively by the teacher. Indiscriminate use may bring about undesirable characteristics and/or neutralize the benefits later when the technique would have a more poignant role in changing behavior.

Advantages or Special Purposes

1. The value of Behavior Modification has been scientifically demonstrated in classroom situations.

2. Behavior Modification is based upon tested principles of learning rather than theory.

3. Since Behavior Modification is concerned with observable, measurable behavior, both the student and teacher are aware of the amount of progress being made.

4. Behavior Modification is applicable to cognitive, affective and kinesthetic learning.

5. The Behavior Modification approach leads to cooperation among the student, teachers, the school, parents, and the mental health professional.

6. Since the emphasis is upon success, a positive atmosphere prevails.

7. The psychological principles involved can readily be learned by the classroom teacher.

8. The academic behaviors specified can be individualized very easily.

Disadvantages or Limitations

1. Not all behaviors to be learned can be measured.

2. Behavior Modification tends to have limitations where long-term retention is desirable.

3. A change in the student may not be based on desired learning but upon the rewards attached.

4. Care must be taken not to unintentionally reward undesirable behaviors.

5. The teacher may become emotionally involved with individuals and lose the effectiveness of the strategy.

6. Some techniques within the behavior modification strategy are extremely time consuming.

7. Behavior Modification requires some individualized type of plan. Giving the same reward to all students will negate the desired effect.

Guidelines for Maximum Utilization

1. Behavior Modification will not accomplish psychologically or academically impossible tasks.

2. The strategy should be used in conjunction with other learning strategies.

3. The behavior must be observable, measurable and controllable.

4. The Behavior Modification strategy must be understood and accepted by peers and parents.

5. The teacher must understand both the limitations and potential of the strategy.

6. After the child learns a new behavior, reinforcement should be tapered off and provided less frequently.

7. Although less reinforcement and reward are needed after the behavior has reached an acceptable level, occasional rewards are necessary to maintain the behavior.

8. Continue to practice the Behavior Modification strategy in numerous settings.

9. Encourage parents to use discriminate reinforcement for events and behavior changes noted in the natural environment of the home.

10. Teach the child to manage its own behavior.

11. A learning environment must be created that will cause the child to engage in desired behaviors.

12. The objectives for each child must be realistic.

13. Introduce changes slowly.

14. The teacher should demonstrate those behaviors that are desired, and not assume that the child knows what to do.

Example

Mrs. Baker had a problem. Her second grade class could not have been less enthused about spelling. She had tried the usual---giving the children who did the poorest lowered grades on their report cards. The low mark and parental pressure had worked in the past, but this class was different. They didn't seem to be that motivated by a low grade. Seeking enlightenment, Mrs. Baker sought out the School Psychologist, Dr. Whizz, and told him of her problem. Sizing up the situation quickly, the good doctor leaned toward Mrs. Baker and said, "Grades are based on the principle of delayed gratification. Children are just learning how to delay rewards---a motivation system specialized in by adults only. Kids want results NOW. Further, a letter grade is very abstract to a child---he can't eat it, or play with it. Until children figure out the game, a grade is just ink on paper. Related to this is the concrete-abstract growth continuum. The younger the person, the more concrete her mental dealings. She wants tangible, hands-on action *and* rewards.

You must admit that spelling is abstract and relatively unimportant to an eight-year-old, besides being a rather boring bit of business. Therefore, it is important for you to set up a system which can make learning how to spell more concrete, more positive, and more tangibly rewarding."

"First, if you're not already doing so, make the spelling words as *real* as possible. Label things in the room. Make up poems with the words, etc. Then, set up a token system in addition to the grades on spelling papers...maybe for every correctly spelled word the child gets one token. At the end of the month children can exchange tokens for items in a *store* you set up with pictures, candy, gum, toys, games, etc. Better still allow them to utilize the tokens to buy time in a game, music, or computer corner, in the comic book library, or arts and crafts corner in your room. You might also consider utilizing cooperative learning and give group rewards for the teams that improve in a collaborative effort. Does this help?"

"Yes, very much," Mrs. Baker replied, "I believe it will work."

And, of course, it did.

Summary

Behavior Modification is a teaching strategy that may be used in regular or special classrooms to modify behavior changes of a specified or desired nature. In its simplest form, it is a procedure whereby the instructor specifies through objectives the desired changes in pupil behavior and, when they occur, a reward is given to the student. In practice, however, it is a systematic process of observing the need for change, determining what changes are desired in each pupil, establishing objectives to carry out the changes and providing reinforcement or rewards for those positive changes made. It must not be used indiscriminately; the program can have negative as well as positive results.

The strategy has been widely tested in laboratory situations and has gradually been deliberately instituted in grade school systems. Positive results have been noted when it has been used by those who know and understand both the positive and negative effects that can result.

The use of this strategy in conjunction with *observation* skills, behavioral objectives, *individualized instruction, case study* and *programmed learning* can stimulate the students toward the desired behavior changes. It has also been used with a large degree of success in *role-playing* and *simulation* activities.

Questions to Promote Discussion

1. As can be readily seen, behavior modification focuses on behavior rather than personality. For example, if you are concerned about a student's tardiness you would say, "Tim, you have been 10-20 minutes late three of the last five school days," rather than, "Tim you are just plain lazy. You never get to school on time." What are likely to be the effects on the student with this focus on behavior rather than on personality?

2. In Behavior Modification, the teacher should demonstrate the desired behavior so that the student will understand what is to be done. This means that the teacher serves as a model of desired behavior. What consequences do you see when you are cast in this model role?

3. What guidelines do you feel should be established concerning the granting of "rewards" for students who demonstrate a desired behavior?

4. What negative results can you expect if you grant rewards improperly to your students?

CASE STUDY

Definition and Description

The Case Study strategy (or case method) is a teaching approach which requires the student to participate actively in problem situations which may be hypothetical or real. The student receives a "case" or report containing pertinent data. The student then analyzes the data, evaluates the nature of the problem, decides upon applicable principles and finally recommends a solution or course of action. The instructor has a wide range of choices of other strategies which may be included in the preparation of a case study technique.

The case may be considered by the class as a whole, by sub-groupings of the class, or on an individual basis. Also, the case may be designed to be handled in variable time formats, ranging from a class period to the entire year.

The case can either be prepared for the student, which means there is a type of *simulation* or *role-playing* aspect of this strategy, or the student can garner his own data first-hand. Data should be objective and devoid of value judgement.

Analysis of the data typically involves the use of reference materials prepared for the study, knowledge, and theory already performed by others and listed in journals and books. It may, however, include *field studies*, personal or group *interview* and *research* activities.

Evaluating and determining applicable principles calls upon the student to make some kind of "reasons-why-this-has-happened" statement based on research or empirical observation. Recommended solutions should be a natural outgrowth of the analysis and evaluation. They should be practical and realistic.

The most common (and, therefore, not displayed here) is the "individual case study," with which most social workers are familiar. It usually involves data on a single person or family, and necessitates that the case worker garner additional pertinent information and recommend appropriate action based on problematic causes.

******

CASE 1:   Weapons Possession at School

Purpose: The purpose of this technique is to add depth to an understanding of human relations. It makes us more aware of the total process an individual goes through as he/she attempts to make decisions about challenging situations, how he/she thinks and feels but does not usually express openly.

Note: A time limit of 30 minutes may need to be established to permit summary discussions to take place with the class as a whole.

Case Setting

This is a meeting of a special task force configured by the superintendent with faculty, student and parent representatives from the ABC School District. It is the first meeting of the group conducted by the county student services supervisor. The problem has been discussed in private by individual members of the staff and faculty, has received recent coverage in the media, and is of considerable concern to the administration as well as parents. The administration is interested in preventing an injurious incident and destructive distractions in the learning environment. The supervisor is aware that the faculty opinions range from a high degree of interest to those who are apathetic. The administration will accept the decision of the task force.

Case Problem

There have been three incidents in the last month involving weapons possession by students. An elementary school child brought his brother's switchblade to school; a middle-school student was found to have a tile-cutter knife in his possession; and a high school student was rumored to have a pistol in his locker, although it was never found.

Case Participants

1. District Student Services Supervisor
2. Elementary teachers (2)
3. Middle school teachers (2)
4. Senior high school teachers (2)
5. Parent representative
6. Student representatives

Task: Discuss the problem and establish a policy (with consequences) for the district.

Case Observers

Observers are those members of the class not participating. They should consider the following questions and concerns, perhaps even developing a written observation sheet to record data for later sharing with the group.

1. How do the participants function as a group?
   a. Conflict
   b. Leadership
   c. Expression of views
   d. Ability to stay on task

2. Problem Solving?
   a. Are the issues and problems made clear?

     b. Do they recognize similarity of issues?

     c. Can they separate them from the problem?

3. Decision-making?
   a. How do they arrive at decisions?
   b. Are the conclusions satisfactory to the participants?
   c. What impedes decision-making?

Summary - For Class Discussion

The participants and observers should be asked for their reactions to and comments on the proceedings, the questions raised and the outcomes and/or alternate solutions. The discussions should emphasize:

a. How productive is the group and why?
b. How did members help to maintain group effectiveness and cohesion?
c. What are the problems and their solutions?
d. How good was the group at problem solving?

******

Advantages or Special Purposes

1. The Case Study approach can provide for individual differences among students.

2. Because the student is involved in a problem situation, interest and motivation are generally high.

3. Active student involvement insures better retention of content as well as practice in effective group skills.

4. The Case Study approach develops responsibility on the part of the learner.

5. Students are invited to develop problem-solving skills in order to arrive at a conclusion to the case.

6. Realistic case studies bridge the gap between the "real" world and that of the school. As an example, the class might choose to study a problem involving their own school organization's operation (lunchroom, playground or class schedules.)

7. Students deal with content on a high cognitive level, learning critical thinking skills in the process.

8. Materials and resources other than the textbook are used in considering the case.

Disadvantages or limitations

1. The Case Study approach can be time consuming.

2. Good case studies are difficult for the teacher to develop in a manageable procedure for the normal size class.

3. Resources and materials needed to pursue the case study successfully are often not available.

4. The teacher must be well prepared for the topic of the study.

5. Students may come to feel that all complex problems have rather simple solutions as experienced in the Case Study.

6. Cases are often what the teacher believes to be important rather than what the students see as important.

7. Cases developed by the students are often controversial and difficult for the teacher to manage, requiring the ancillary teaching of group or collaborative skills which takes additional time.

8. Evaluation is difficult due to the open discussion or forum approach for group cases.

Guidelines for Maximum Utilization

1. Cases should be explicitly and unambiguously written.

2. Cases should be written to fit the level of the students in terms of maturity and problem-solving skills.

3. Students should be presented with several similar cases prior to permitting the students to select their own cases.

4. A check must be made to insure that materials and resources dealing with the case are available.

5. Check on students periodically to insure that they are progressing in a desirable direction. Develop a check list of proposed duties or task items to help the group be successful.

6. Resist the temptation to solve the student's case. Let the student handle the case in order to benefit from the activity.

7. Establish a method and procedure for periodic and final evaluation prior to beginning the Case Study strategy.

8. Assist the students in evaluating the experience in terms of the content and processes involved.

9. In cases that deal with controversial topics, clear the activity with the school administration prior to beginning the use of this strategy.

10. Be prepared to teach collaborative skills necessary for successful Case Study group work, i.e. disagreeing in an agreeable way, sharing support, accepting and liking others, etc.

11. Attempt to include other strategies such as *role-playing, simulation, interview,* and *questioning* within the structure of the Case Study.

Summary

The Case Study method is another approach to active learning in individual, group and class settings. Through the use of hypothetical, but realistic, situations the student has the opportunity to use problem-solving approaches that are meaningful and understandable. It requires the student to collect data, analyze it, and make suggestions or recommendations for decision-making. The project may be simple in the beginning and lead to the more complex with the student gaining experience in these learning processes. Case Study can also be used effectively as a subordinate strategy in *cooperative learning* situations by having some students assume roles such as reporter, checker, encourager, etc.

Using the Case Study strategy can, if it is properly directed, assist in the solving of school or community problems. The community sees the student working on topics that are of wide interest in the community and thus has greater respect for the educational programs at the local school. It further provides an opportunity to resolve attitudinal conflicts in the community.

Case Study is not a strategy to be used indiscriminately. It requires careful planning, specific objectives, clearly specified guidelines, and a precise means of evaluation. The teacher can and must expect to be available for individual assistance and must insure that materials, equipment and resources are readily available to the students. As with all other strategies, the school administration should be aware of the project and give the support to ventures which take the pupil outside the normal school environment.

Questions to Promote Discussion

1. What do you consider to be the major difficulty in using the Case Study?

2. What suggestions do you have for overcoming this major difficulty?

3. What, if anything, do the observers learn when the Case Study is used?

4. What do you consider to be the best use of the Case Study? Why?

5. How might working in groups help broaden the context of this strategy?

COMMUNITY RESOURCES

Definition and Description

Basically, Community Resources include any activity outside the school which has educational use. Included, then, are *people, places,* and *things* found in the community which the teacher can use to facilitate learning.

The resource, although located outside the school building itself, may be brought to the school, or the class may go to the site to carry out a planned activity. Often an elder citizen of the community can enhance the study of history or biology, art, folk dancing and literature. Members of the business community, health care industry or manufacturing companies are all potential resources. An insignificant dried up canal or creek bed can bring a wide variety of activities into focus. For example, a canal stream can be used to study the history, trade, transportation and economy of the past. It can also be used to study the plant life, become a collection area for artifacts, or be used as a model for the construction of science and art projects. The resources of the community are limited only by the imagination of the teacher and class. (See *field study* and *interview.*)

Advantages and Special Purposes

1. The use of Community Resources can bring the school and community closer together.

2. Community Resources can provide the student with first-hand knowledge and experience which facilitate more practical learning and better retention of information.

3. The use of Community Resources adds authenticity to learning since it involves contact with real people, places or things outside the classroom walls.

4. Interaction between the school and community enables the student to develop a broader understanding of the community.

5. The use of Community Resources adds excitement to learning, placing it in the context of an "expedition" to explore academic content in a relevant way.

6. Community Resources are applicable to all types of learning: cognitive, affective, and kinesthetic.

7. Students can develop social skills in helping plan and use Community Resources.

8. Students can assist in the selection of Community Resources as a decision-making experience.

9. Members of the community are generally willing to devote time and energy to these types of activities.

10. Community Resource activities are inexpensive and within the budgets of most schools.

11. Technology, i.e. computers, fax machines, modems and interactive media, makes the whole world a potential community resource, limited only by one's imagination.

Disadvantages or Limitations

1. Specific Community Resources are sometimes difficult to locate and/or schedule.

2. To use certain Community Resources, teachers must often obtain prior administrative and/or parental approval.

3.   People used as Community Resources often do not know how to transfer their knowledge and information to youth.

4.   Field trips into the community are often overlooked due to factors such as student safety, control, expense and teacher liability.

5.   Improper use or planning for use of Community Resources can impede learning and create conflict between the school and community.

6.   Proper planning for utilizing Community Resources is time consuming and potentially frustrating due to legal and financial concerns.

7.   The teachings of the community can run counter to the teachings of the school.

8.   Since the teacher is dependent on agents of the community with primary responsibilities not essential to education, last-minute cancellations often occur, leaving the teacher stranded.

9.   Rural areas may be handicapped by lack of access to museums, parks, business and industrial sites. Likewise, urban students will have limited access to the more rural types of Community Resources.

Guidelines for Maximum Utilization

1.   Plan! Plan! Plan! Begin by developing a file of people, places and things in the community or in nearby areas which can be used to enhance instruction.

2.   Remember to ask other faculty/staff for their ideas, and consider combining classes to maximize effectiveness, i.e. the use of curricular thematic units.

3. Check each possible resource well in advance of its use. When using individuals as "amateur" guest speakers, consider coaching them regarding the best ways to relate to your students.

4. Develop a resource file with information concerning procedures for use, necessary arrangements, people to contact, times the resources are available, size of groups that can be accommodated, etc., for each resource considered.

5. Investigate all legal, financial and economic factors involved for each resource considered. Parental permission forms may need to be obtained for off campus trips.

6. Include the planned use of the resource in the total lesson or unit of study. Consider inviting interested parents and your administrator to join your class.

7. Present, in writing, the total unit or lesson to your administrator for approval. Having the plan in writing helps the administrator give approval and helps you plan more effectively.

8. Design a Plan B, in case of last-minute cancellations.

9. Upon completion of the lesson or unit, evaluate the resource utilized and place that information in the file for future use.

10. Incorporate the knowledge gained into the curriculum or lesson conclusions.

11. Don't forget to have the students send notes of gratitude to those persons who made the resource available. This can be an excellent creative and social skill-building activity.

Example

I.   A teacher advertised through an article in the paper for volunteers with various areas of expertise, hobbies, knowledge, etc., who would be willing to contribute an hour a week during the term.   When she had screened the applicants, she furnished a list to her class to see who was interested in which area.   As it turned out they were rather varied:

    4 German Language
    6 Chemistry
    7 Photography
    5 Arts and Crafts
    6 Electronics

    Each week the resource people came and took their "little brood" aside for intriguing projects and pastimes.

II.   Another teacher did approximately the same thing, but had the whole class choose one area for a month, and had the resource person in once a week for four or five weeks.   Areas included: inventions, movie-making, archaeology, video-taping, music, hypnotism, fortune-telling, scuba diving, veterinary science, computers, etc.

    The first session was spent in establishing interests of the students in the area and a set of goal expectations based on these interests (and, or course, the expertise and resources of the guest instructor).   Part of the final session was spent in evaluating the accomplishment of goals. Reports of new learnings were prepared by students and were sent home to parents. (See *interest centers*.)

Summary

    Community Resources have an inherent place in the curriculum of all schools, but they are often overlooked as a teaching tool in many educational systems.   Major industries, parks, museum and historical monuments are obvious places to visit, but consider the people and places that are not nationally known but have a high educational value?

The teacher does not have to leave the school property to find a true resource. In many instances, teachers and other employees within the system have traveled and taken hundreds of slides and snapshots or brought back many souvenirs which if used could add new dimensions to the learning-teaching processes. Studies of the environment can be undertaken by studying the playground and surrounding areas. Sociological studies can be made by observing the people in action in or near the school. With a little imagination, even the classroom can be a resource.

Normally a community resource is considered to be something away from the school to visit, but in many instances it means bringing a person or exhibit to the school. Regardless of the definition, it is a tool that can provide new learning experiences to the class and assist the teacher in making lessons more meaningful and with lasting effects.

Community Resources, like all other teaching strategies, require advance consideration, study and preparation before they can become the meaningful tool they were designed to be. Begin early to note places of interest that will enhance the lesson. Make notes regarding the cost and the time needed to tour or complete the activity. Jot down the names of key individuals for contact and scheduling. Be knowledgeable about the procedures and requirements with the school for making use of Community Resources. Above all, have the objectives for using the resource firmly in mind to ensure that the lesson is meaningful.

Questions to Promote Discussion

1. What are some reasons why Community Resources are so seldom used as a teaching strategy?

2. List some ways of overcoming the reasons you stated in answer to Question #1.

3. The present emphasis on school-business partnerships may well increase the use of Community Resources. If so, in what ways?

4. What advice concerning proper use of this strategy would you give to a teacher who has not previously used this approach?

5. How could you involve colleagues in this strategy, and what benefits might that have?

CONTRACTING

Definition and Description

Contracting is a device in which a student (or a *cooperative learning* group) and teacher together write exactly what is to be accomplished, in what period of time, and for what grade or reward. The objectives are clearly specified, the work objectives outlined, and both teacher and student(s) sign the written agreement known as a "contract." Two copies are prepared so that the teacher and pupil can each keep one for reference and records. The contract itself is a written set of varied learning situations. Some are common to the entire class, a group, or individualized to meet the needs of a student.

To initiate the teacher in contract writing, a sample is provided. It should be modified to meet specific needs.

******
PERFORMANCE CONTRACT

For a Course in _____ Human Development _____

Name _____ Joe Dogood _____ Date ___ 3/24/93 _____

For the grade circled below, I/we am going to:	To exhibit my progress of these requirements, I/we will:

A - Do an original research project as explained on the attached sheet, plus completing all items for grade B, C, and D.
Submit the outline of my paper to the teacher by
_____ and the completed paper by_____.

    (Date)   (Date)

B - Perform a case study as explained on the attached sheet
Submit the case study to the teacher by _____.
                                                    (Date)
plus completing all items for grade C and D.

C - Visit one of the following places and report my observations, plus
completing the materials items for grade D. (a. Elementary School,
b. High School, c. Mental Hospital-youth wing, d. Juvenile
Detention Center)
Submit a 1-page handwritten personal reaction paper to the teacher
by _____.
      (Date)

D - Read text of the course, *Human Development* and pass three (3)
examinations; Be in class attendance 90 percent of the time; and,
Write a one-page report on a topic of interest from the text. Passed
examinations on:

_____   _____   _____
   (Date)   (Date)   (Date)

All exams and reports are graded pass or fail. If failed, they may be
repeated. Please allow flexibility in your schedule.

_____   _____
Date   Student(s)

_____   _____
Date   Teacher

_____   _____
Date   Parent (Optional)

******

Notice that in order to get a D in this course, the student must read
the text, write a one-page report, and get a "pass" on three exams. In
order to get a C, he/she must perform the requirements for that grade plus
all requirements for the next lower grade. The same holds true for the

grade of B. If a student signs a contract for an A at the beginning of the semester but for some reason completes only the requirements for a B, he/she would get credit for what has been accomplished.

Advantages or Special Purposes

1. The emphasis is on learning and success rather than testing and failure.

2. Students have a self-controlled opportunity for independence in their learning activities.

3. The relationship between students and instructor is improved because the student is not trying to "out-psych" the teacher, reducing or eliminating behavior problems.

4. Cheating and duty-shirking are reduced.

5. The conditions for achieving a grade are clearly understood.

6. Communication is optimized as student and teacher *must* meet in regular individual conferences.

7. The learning objectives are clear to everyone.

8. Students can help select the projects rather than having the teacher pre-select the topic.

9. Varied experiences are ensured. Students do not just "do more of the same activity" for a higher grade.

10. Students have choices, exercise decision-making abilities, and learn to organize and manage time.

11. Students may try and try again if they have difficulty.

12. Contracting in groups distributes the workload, allows group members to share knowledge and to receive support. Individuals still receive a grade plus the opportunity to earn bonus points if the group does well.

Disadvantages or Limitations

1. It is more work initially for the instructor than the *lecture* followed by a testing period.

2. Students can settle for grades below their "potential" which, perhaps, should be their choice.

3. More record monitoring is necessary to ensure that the students are keeping up with their schedules and are not having difficulties. This becomes necessary if the students have become accustomed to educational spoon-feeding of structure in the past.

4. "Quantity" may tend to replace "quality" as a criterion.

5. The contract requires both in-school and out-of-school resources, which may be difficult to locate.

6. Some students may lack the self-motivation required to fulfill the contract responsibilities.

Guidelines for Maximum Utilization

1. Preparation of objectives must always come first. What do you wish the student to learn academically? Socially? What does the student wish to learn? What are the best methods to achieve the objectives? What are the best criteria to use in judging whether the student has achieved the objectives?

2. Ensure that all materials, resource people and places necessary to fulfill the contract are available.

3. Draw up contracts based on Items 1 and 2 of the guidelines.

4. When you have your contractual agreement sessions, students must understand the necessity of self-motivation, time schedules and material needs. Include adequate time for "re-trials" in the event that students are not successful on tests and reports.

5. Remember, the contract does not eliminate the need for daily class activities, but it is supplemental to regular class work.

6. Clearly establish the level of acceptance on papers and exams. Since students get either a "pass" or "fail" on tests, you need to determine the pass-fail line (75%, 80%, etc.).

7. Once the contract is signed, it is binding upon both the teacher and student or group. Keep your word.

8. As a result of experiences, revise your procedures, contracts, objectives, etc. Continuously sharpen up the process and keep it updated.

9. Before beginning this strategy, be certain it has the approval of the school administration.

20. Repeated use of this strategy for every lesson or unit will weaken its effectiveness. Attempt to use it in selective situations and blend the use of other strategies within the contract.

Summary

The Contracting strategy is a stepping-stone into the individualized learning processes (as well as effective in *cooperative learning* groups). The contract is written to meet the needs of each individual, based on objectives of both the student and the teacher. The level of acceptable achievement must be based on more than the general expectations of the class. Consideration must include the maturity of the students, previous experiences in contracting, the ability to carry out tasks on an individual basis, and the challenge to both the teacher and the students. Contracting is not a strategy that, once assigned, leaves the teacher free from all daily planning and teaching. Quite the contrary, it requires the teacher to monitor progress through individual conferences, to assist students in finding the needed resources, and to keep regular records of attendance, progress and testing. In *cooperative learning* groups the role of "checker" may be utilized to fulfill this function and to keep members on track.

The contract can be an elaborate document or a simple written statement of agreement between the student and/or the students with each other, and the teacher. The important part of this strategy is the opportunity it provides students to learn while doing a project they have selected. It is a chance for the student to experience success and failure, yet provides the opportunity to try again with a challenged feeling rather than that of complete failure. In the group situation with effective collaborative skills in place, the members of the group will not want to let the group down and will benefit from the extra encouragement and support.

It is important to clearly establish administrative approval before beginning this strategy. Since some of the contracts may require leaving the school environs to visit a community resource, parents should also be aware of the activity and understand the concept of contracting. With parental support and administrative approval, the teacher ensures positive chances of success.

Questions to Promote Discussion

1. Luke Lance is going to teach the sixth grade in a school system which utilizes the self-contained classroom. Luke wants to try contracting. Do you recommend that Luke begin the method with one specific subject or with all subjects at the same time?

2. You have decided to use contracting and all involved people agree it is a good idea. Upon implementing the approach, your best student decides to settle for a C. What would be your reaction? What would you do?

3. Also, in Problem 2, your most "marginal" student decides to shoot for an A. What would be your reaction? What would you do?

4. In facing the situations in Problems 2 and 3 above, were you consistent? In what ways? Did any inconsistencies appear in your thinking? If so, what were they?

5. In constructing group contracts, what precautionary steps would you take?

COOPERATIVE LEARNING

Definition and Description

Cooperative Learning is not new; it has been around since the early 1900's when it was used in one room school houses. During the 1950's, educators moved away from cooperation toward a model of individualization and competition with the result being a student deficit in the skills necessary to work effectively with one another, accept each other's differences, resolve conflicts, and pool their resources to solve complex problems. In our contemporary society, business and industry are finding a need to return to the concept of cooperation and team building if they are to be competitive in today's global economy. Millions of dollars annually are being spent in the re-training of employees to take more initiative, assume more responsibility in the day to day business operations, and be more cooperative with fellow workers. Our future work force attends schools today. As educators, it behooves us to help prepare those future employees for the world they will live, work, and play in as the 21st Century draws near. The importance of Cooperative Learning cannot be overemphasized.

Two basic models of Cooperative Learning are popular today. The directed teaching models developed by Spencer Kagan and Robert Slavin in which specific teaching methods ("recipes") or structures are described and presented, then adapted for use at different grade levels. The conceptual model, which takes longer to learn and understand, has been developed by such authors as David and Roger Johnson and Elizabeth Cohen. Much of the information described here has been taken from the conceptual model of David and Roger Johnson.

All models utilize the basic elements of positive interdependence, individual accountability, collaborative/social skills, and group processing. The teacher's role in Cooperative Learning changes from being in front of the students doing most of the talking (and most of the work) to becoming a facilitator who guides student learning in both academic as well as the social realm. **Cooperative Learning may best be defined as small heterogeneously mixed working groups of students learning collaborative/social skills while working toward a common academic goal or task.**

Advantages or Special Purposes

1. Students learn from one another, learn the material covered at a deeper level and feel better about themselves and their interactions with their peers.

2. Cooperative Learning can be used successfully with a variety of other teaching strategies.

3. Students learn valuable social skills such as resolving conflict, problem solving, criticizing ideas and not people, paraphrasing, asking questions, giving direction to the group's work, and building on each other's information.

4. Students learn trust building, communication and leadership skills from which they benefit for the rest of their lives in the work place, or in relationships.

5. Students usually enjoy working together because they are actively involved in the learning process.

6. The teacher's role changes from being in the front of the room doing most of the work and all of the talking, to being a facilitator of student learning, monitoring and collecting data on student performance, as well as intervening when the group needs assistance in doing the task or learning to work together more effectively.

7. Cooperative Learning efficacy is heavily supported by over 90 years of research found in over 650 studies.

8. When in place, processing skills help students learn effective conflict resolution which improves group functioning in the future.

9. Helping students learn to cooperate in their groups gives them valuable life-long learning skills.

10. Teachers will eventually be able to cover more material at a deeper level with students who will also enjoy the learning process.

Disadvantages or Limitations

1. Learning to facilitate Cooperative Learning expertly requires training, experience, and perseverance. It may take 2 to 3 years before a teacher can use these techniques routinely.

2. Giving group grades before collaborative skills are in place creates some problems for teachers, students and their parents.

3. Groups finish work at different times. Sometimes students argue or refuse to do the work. Some students don't know how to get along with others and settle their differences. Some students want to work alone.

4. Initially, the teaching of collaborative/social skills takes up a great deal of class time, affecting the amount of content covered.

5. Some students do not like to work in groups. If individual accountability is not in place, some students do all of the work and the other group members let them.

6. Cooperative Learning does not work well in easy lessons.

7. Processing skills take time to learn and to carry out in the classroom. Conflicts may arise for which the teacher may not be prepared.

8. Working in cooperative groups creates a level of "noise" that may be uncomfortable for some teachers.

Guidelines for Maximum Utilization

The teacher should understand the basic elements of a good Cooperative Learning lesson before attempting to do Cooperative Learning in their classrooms.

1. Create a sense of positive interdependence in the groups so that students feel mutually connected to each other. This may be done by:
   a. Structuring a group goal or task that all group members must work toward, such as completing a single product or paper that is representative of the group's efforts.
   b. Assigning individual roles such as reader, recorder, checker, encourager, noise monitor, or materials "getter." These roles specify responsibilities the group needs to complete in order to accomplish the task.
   c. Structuring group rewards or bonus points that provide incentive for working together. Everyone is rewarded or no one is rewarded.
   d. Creating an "outside enemy" where groups are in friendly competition with each other, scores from past groups, or the clock.
   e. Limiting the resources (such as using only one book, one pencil, or one worksheet) in the group so that they must be shared.
   f. Creating a physical environment (such as moving desks close together, sitting on the floor in a certain section of the room, or sitting at one end of a table) where the group is designated to work together so they are positioned knee to knee and eye to eye.

g.   Structuring a division of labor in the task so that one part of the work must be done before the next part is started.

h.   Creating an identity in the group (such as developing a group name, motto, cheer, logo, or flag) that makes the group unique and creates a sense of belonging and connectedness.

i.   Creating a fantasy situation where students imagine they are in a life or death emergency (such as deciding how to survive after being stranded on the moon, in the desert, or in the frozen tundra as a result of a plane crash or shipwreck) or must deal with problems (such as pretending to be the world's best scientists whose task is to end world hunger) that are serious, but not real. (See *Simulation*.)

2.   Another essential element of Cooperative Learning is the structuring of individual accountability in the groups. This helps to prevent group members from "hitchhiking" and not doing their share of the work. There are several means by which teachers can structure individual accountability in their cooperative groups. They may randomly call on one or more members of the group to give and explain the group's answers, or give an individual exam or quiz on the material covered by the group. Other ways include asking all group members to sign their signatures to the group's work indicating their agreement with the group's answers, having members use different colored pens for writing their individual answers, or randomly selecting one worksheet from the group for evaluation.

3.   A third essential element of Cooperative Learning is the teaching of interpersonal and small group skills. These skills are necessary for students to learn and use if the group is to collaborate, resolve conflict, enjoy working together, and effectively and efficiently perform the tasks asked of them. These collaborative, small group social skills (such as communication, leadership, trust-building, conflict management, and decision making skills) need to be taught as precisely and

purposely as any other academic skills. A T-Chart is one effective way to teach collaborative skills. The teacher also needs to collect data regarding the students' use of these skills on an observation sheet for giving feedback to the group during the processing. Students must see the need for using the skills, be taught how to do them, and then be given ample opportunities for practice and perseverance in using the skills until they are internalized. This can be time consuming and frustrating.

4. The final basic element in Cooperative Learning deals with processing the group's effectiveness in using the prescribed social/collaborative skills and how well they accomplished the academic task assigned. This is a time of reflection for the teacher and the group. If students are to learn from their experience in working together, they must reflect on that experience. Unexamined experience rarely benefits anyone. Common processing questions include: Did we do what we were supposed to do? What did we do well? What do we need to improve on? Were we concerned about maintaining the relationships in our group? What helped us to be successful? What hindered us? What do we need to do differently next time in order to be a more effective group? The group or class may then decide to set goals for being more productive in the future. A formal processing form where group members write down their suggestions is helpful. Less formal or verbal forms of processing are also valuable. Either way, processing what happened needs to be done if the groups are to become more effective in the future in their use of collaborative skills and ability to accomplish the assigned tasks. Processing, due to lack of time in a busy school schedule, is often neglected. It is one of the key ingredients that helps groups solve problems and conflicts, better organize their work, and build more meaningful relationships in the group. Processing should not be neglected.

5. Some thoughts on Grouping: Structuring heterogeneity in groups according to age, ability, gender, and culture helps

students accept diversity, view problems from different perspectives and learning styles, and see different ways of using social skills. Optimum group size varies from 2 to 4 members, depending on the age of the students, their ability to use social skills, the time available, and the difficulty of the material to be covered.   Young children, short time availability, and handicapping conditions necessitate the use of smaller groups, usually pairs. Larger groups may be used with older students, when there is more difficult or abstract material to be learned, and when there is more time available.

There are 3 basic types of Cooperative Learning groups; *base, formal* and *informal. Base groups* are structured after the teacher knows the students and can choose the most socially isolated students in the classroom. These students are then placed in groups with 2 or 3 supportive, caring, and task-oriented students. The function of base groups is mostly for social support. They meet on a regular basis and remain intact for 9 weeks, a semester, an entire school year, or longer. Advisor and advisee or AODA groups are good examples of where the base group philosophy would work well. *Formal groups* may be randomly chosen or assigned by the teacher based on academic ability, with a high, medium and low achieving student in each group. These groups stay together for a curriculum unit in length, approximately 2-3 weeks. *Informal groups* are randomly selected by the teacher using any number of methods, counting off in authors, scientists, a foreign language, birthday months, size of shoes, color of eyes or clothing, dots on the backs of chairs, M & M's, colored strips of paper handed out when students arrive, parts of speech, or a puzzle, favorite color, sport or singer, etc. Informal groups stay together for a day or two. The message to the students is that they will get to work with everyone in the class sooner or later. One rule of thumb: Do not change groups just because students do not get along with each other. This may send the wrong message to students about learning to use the skills we are trying to teach them. Often group members that struggle through personality conflicts successfully end up with a very bonded, and connected group having learned valuable social skills in the process!

Summary

Cooperative Learning is not the easiest way to teach, but when used effectively, will help students be better learners, praise and support each other's learning, and develop necessary social/collaborative skills for use in problem solving. Teaching students to work cooperatively will help prepare them for the world of work and the team building necessary to succeed. Creating a sense of positive interdependence within the groups helps the members feel connected to each other and their learning.

To be an effective teacher of Cooperative Learning requires time, training, practice and support from colleagues, parents, and administration. It is best to go slowly, be well prepared, and let Cooperative Learning evolve into a teaching style. Most of all...enjoy the process!

Questions to Promote Discussion

1. Cooperative Learning works best in situations where many and varied answers are expected. What areas of your curriculum lend themselves to use with Cooperative Learning groups?

2. The teacher's role in using Cooperative Learning changes from being "the sage on the stage" to being a facilitator. How do you feel about that? How will that change what you do in your classroom? What will you do about grading?

3. Children are not born with the skills to interact effectively with others. They must be taught to do so. What collaborative skills do your students need? How will you teach these skills?

DEMONSTRATION

Definition and Description

Demonstration is the process wherein one person (or a small group) does something in the presence of others in order to show them how to do it or to illustrate a principle. Demonstration utilizes both auditory and visual means of communication.

Advantages or Special Purposes

1. Demonstration adds to learning by giving students the opportunity to see and hear what is actually happening.

2. Demonstration can be used to illustrate ideas, principles, and concepts for which words are inadequate

3. *Good* Demonstrations hold the learner's attention.

4. Demonstrations can be financially economical as only the demonstrator needs materials.

5. Students can conduct Demonstrations, thus building associated skills and attitudes.

6. Demonstrations can reduce hazards before students begin experimentation or operation with materials involved (especially in science labs, shops, or family living classes).

7. Demonstrations lead to a reduction in the length of trial-and-error time.

8. Good Demonstrations set performance standards (which can be inspiring in such areas as the arts, music, computer labs, physical education, etc.).

9. Demonstration is especially beneficial in the area of skills.

10. Demonstration is an excellent technique for utilizing community resource persons which in turn is good for public relations.

Disadvantages or Limitations

1. Demonstration can require much planning and preparation by the demonstrator.

2. A Demonstration can be ineffective if the demonstrator only "shows and tells," without active feedback.

3. The Demonstration approach cannot be properly used in large classrooms or with extremely small objects because all students cannot see.

4. If the audio portion of the Demonstration does not fit (flow with) the visual portion, it can confuse the student.

5. Demonstration can lead to imitation without understanding.

6. Demonstration can lead to "oversimplification" of the complex, which can result in feelings of failure or inferiority when students cannot "measure up."

7. Demonstration is difficult to use with affective and higher-level cognitive learnings.

8. Several Demonstrations become time consuming.

Guidelines for Maximum Utilization

1. Spend the necessary time to plan and develop the needed materials for the Demonstration.

2. Practice or rehearse the Demonstration in its entirety with an eye on time limitations.

3. When it is time to perform the Demonstration check that all materials are at hand.

4. Establish appropriate seating arrangements so that the entire audience can see and hear.

5. Utilize questions during the Demonstration to provide feedback.

6. It often helps to discuss and demonstrate the "wrong way" to perform a task as well as the "right way" (e.g., "Look what happens when too much water is added while forming this ceramic pot on the wheel.").

7. At the conclusion of the Demonstration, conduct a brief review of the steps involved or a short summary of what has happened.

8. If feasible, have a student or group replicate the Demonstration.

Summary

One of the greatest benefits of Demonstration is showing how something is accomplished properly or expertly. Naturally, the Demonstration should be properly prepared to ensure that this goal is achieved. A good Demonstration inspires, a poor one distracts and demotivates.

Demonstration is especially useful in the arts, music, science, mathematics, and athletics. It is commonly used in conjunction with a short explanatory *lecture*.

Questions to Promote Discussion

1. Why is a good Demonstration a really powerful means of teaching?

2. In your estimation, in what way is Demonstration often misused?

3. What do you consider to be the key element in using Demonstration properly? Why?

4. What are areas in the curriculum where demonstrations would be appropriate?

DISCOVERY

Definition and Description

Discovery is a term which connotes different meanings to different people. Basically, Discovery is a teaching strategy which enables students to find the answers themselves. In Discovery students are involved in learning how to learn.

In practice, directed Discovery is used more than pure Discovery since the teacher generally creates the conditions under which the "discovery" is to occur. In essence, "discovery" is really "re-discovery," as the intent is that students will discover for themselves that which has been previously discovered.

In implementing Discovery, the teacher creates a situation in which the student is faced with a problem. In solving the problem, the student uses raw data and behaves in the manner required by the nature of the discipline and the problem. Thus, the student studies history the same way that a historian does or as a biologist studies biology.

Advantages or Special Purposes

1. Since the student actively discovers the information, knowledge retention will be increased.

2. Discovery helps the student learn how to follow leads and clues, and to record findings, thus equipping him/her to handle new problematic situations.

3. The rewards inherent in discovering something provide the student with intrinsic motivation.

4. The student develops further interest in what is being studied.

5.   Students develop the skills and attitudes essential for self-directed learning.

6.   Students develop a deeper understanding of the tasks of a scholar.

7.   Discovery operates at the higher levels of the cognitive domain (analysis, synthesis, etc.); it also encourages intuitive thinking.

8.   The pupil is provided with numerous opportunities to draw inferences from data by critical thinking, either inductive or deductive.

Disadvantages or Limitations

1.   Permitting students to discover their own knowledge is very time consuming. It is usually inefficient to expect students to re-discover or recreate all knowledge required in an area.

2.   Many textbooks and materials available to the teacher are written for exposition rather than Discovery.

3.   The student often gets bogged down or loses direction before the problem is solved.

4.   Students often discover things other than what was intended to be "discovered."

5.   A non-productive Discovery following great effort can be extremely deflating for the student.

6.   The teacher must have a strong background in the subject to handle unexpected discoveries.

7.   Some students just seem unable to make the intended Discovery.

Guidelines for Maximum Utilization

1. Discovery should be used only when you have enough subject matter mastery to handle unexpected "discoveries."

2. The depth of information to be handled and the time needed for the Discovery must be gauged in terms of the student's skill level and maturation and the objectives of the course or subject.

3. Setting up the problem and the conditions for Discovery requires detailed and thorough planning.

4. Be certain that proper materials and raw data are available.

5. Be open to problems as they arise and be willing to learn along with the students.

6. Upon conclusion of the Discovery experience, spend time reviewing and/or processing the experience in terms of both the knowledge learned and the processes involved.

7. Permit students to share discoveries with the class to extend the learning environment.

Example

To give the class an opportunity to use Discovery, in learning of value-processes, present the following situation to small groups within the class. It is a form of *simulation* but requires the student to use data, accept or reject positions of others and arrive at a conclusion.

HOSPITAL ADVISORY BOARD

You are a Hospital Advisory Board. There is one heart available to your hospital for transplanting, but you have ten people on the ward who must receive the heart or they will die. But, of course, *only one can live.*

Your task: Select the one who will live (or the nine who will die).

A.   Male Heart Surgeon; Age 55; Married; No children.
B.   Male Insurance Salesman; Age 32; Married; 2 Children.
C.   Male College drop-out; Age 20; Single.
D.   Female Hispanic Elementary School Teacher; Age 27; Married; 1 Child.
E.   Nigerian Minister; Age 58; Married; Children Grown-up.
F.   16 year-old Girl
G.   Female Militant; Divorced;Age 26; 2 Children.
H.   Male Asian College Student; Age 22; Married; No Children.
I.   Iranian Air Force Colonel; Age 49; Single.
J.   Male Politician; Age 36; Married; 4 Children.

Procedure:

1.   Allow individuals 5 minutes to rank-order choices prior to group involvement.

2.   Use any method of selection your group decides upon together.

3.   Rank-order all ten candidates with #1 being the one that should receive the heart first. That way, if #1 cannot use the heart for some reason, you will have a second choice ready immediately. The last one on the list should be, in your minds, the last one to be "saved."

4.   Turn in one paper with your signatures indicating consensus.

5.   Explain why you chose #1 as you did. Please be specific about criteria utilized.

Sample Follow-Up Questions for the Teacher

1.   How much time was wasted fighting the problem? What implication does this have for our everyday lives?

2. What prejudices surfaced?

3. Was there "sense" in establishing the selection criteria?

4. Was the selection process humanely done?

5. Did a leader evolve in the group?

6. Was the leader fair (unbiased)?

7. What comments made during the simulation turned you off?

8. Who used good collaborative skills to help the group perform its task? What did they do?

Summary

The thrust of Discovery, as with the Socratic method is that answers, or the potential for discovering answers, are inherent within the student. This strategy transforms the teacher position to one of "guide on the side" rather than "sage on the stage"---requiring the teacher to guide the process patiently until the "revelation" occurs. A very good example is illustrated in Postman and Weingardner's *Teaching as a Subversive Activity* (although the example is labeled "Inquiry"). A social studies teacher brings a small black briefcase to class, explaining that it is the world's smallest computer, and that it will answer any question the students ask, but only one. An earnest discussion (that lasted for days) ensued as to which question to ask. Values had to be shared, attitudes and ideas exchanged, and priorities arrived at to determine *the* question. Once the teacher had "set the stage," it was the students' show and the teacher merely acted as a social and structural referee.

Discovery is frequently used in science and math but is relevant for most other subject areas as well. The teacher provides the materials and the students provide the discovering. Some pure form Discovery strategists accept all discoveries, stating that there is no *right* answer.

Discovery is a process approach as opposed to the usual product-oriented emphasis in education.

Questions to Promote Discussion

1. What is the major advantage of the Discovery approach? Explain.

2. What is the chief limitation of the Discovery approach? Why?

3. How would you attempt to overcome the limitation cited in response to Question #2?

4. What collaborative skills could be taught to assist the groups in functioning more effectively?

5. What areas of your curricular interest lend themselves to the Discovery approach?

DISCUSSION

Definition and Description

The *Dictionary of Education* describes Discussion as "an activity in which people talk together in order to share information about a topic or problem or to seek possible available evidence or a solution...."

Discussion may be implemented in a variety of ways. The types of Discussion available to the teacher include whole-class discussions, debates, panels, buzz-sessions, and forums. Each type has its own characteristics.

The *whole-class* Discussion is the type generally referred to when teachers employ the discussion method. The teacher simply leads an informal Discussion involving the class as a whole. The teacher, as the director of the Discussion, asks questions, clarifies student comments, and makes tentative summaries to help students achieve understanding of the topic.

Debate is generally used in the classroom as a small-group technique, with a small number of students teamed on either side of an issue. Each team is given a specific amount of time to present its "side" of the issue. The members can alternate presentations and often are identified as "pro" and "con" with respect to the issue. Rebuttals of a specific time duration then follow the presentations. Upon conclusion of the debate, the teacher can enter into a whole-class discussion on the issue.

Position Reversal Debate is similar to debate, except both groups are required to take notes on the other team's "position presentation." Teams then switch positions and debate the other point of view using the notes. They then work on solving the problem that started the debate utilizing vantage points from both points of view. This discussion format helps students develop conflict resolution, problem solving, and consensus building skills.

In utilizing *panels*, the teacher can divide the class into groups of three to six students. The students comprising the panel then organize themselves, research the topic, discuss their data, and present their findings, leading into a whole-class discussion.

In *buzz sessions*, students are placed in small groups for a specific amount of time to discuss a given issue or topic. Reports of the results of the various buzz groups are then presented to the entire class and stimulate whole-class discussion.

The *forum* is a specific Discussion type in which a small number of students present information to the larger group. Upon the conclusion of the presentation, the presenters then solicit questions on the topic from the audience. This places the presenters in the role of "authorities" on the topic and questions may be directed to specific members of the group of "experts."

In *discrepant discussion* the teacher presents unusual or opposing viewpoints, and students work in small groups to refute or defend them.

The types of Discussion approaches listed above represent only the most commonly used. Each of the types presented can be used in either a modified form or in combination with each other. Whatever the case, teachers should use the approach properly in terms of its inherent characteristics.

Advantages or Special Purposes

1. Students learn through Discussion. Not only do students learn the cognitive information considered, they utilize the information in a meaningful manner and thus develop critical thinking and problem solving skills.

2. Discussion techniques get at attitude development. By engaging in meaningful discussion with fellow students, a given student finds his/her own values and beliefs challenged. Such

a finding can lead to significant self-awareness and attitudinal change on the part of the student.

3. Discussion provides the student with the opportunity to develop questioning skills and responses. It offers an opportunity to develop organization and formulation of answers. In essence, the student begins to think and organize on his/her feet.

4. The proper use of Discussion can aid the student in the development of a positive self-concept.

5. The student is free to offer or not to offer comment.

6. Discussion has a positive effect upon the mental activity of the student. Since the role of the student is not as passive as with some other approaches, the student maintains a high degree of mental alertness. This alertness is one reason why discussion is often praised as being a motivator.

7. Discussion provides the teacher with information about the student which can aid in a better understanding of students, individually and collectively. Careful observation of the behavior of students in group activities provides the teacher with much information related to the social, psychological, emotional, and skill development of the student.

Disadvantages or Limitations

1. Discussion activities are usually time consuming compared with more direct approaches.

2. Discussions often break down, lag, or become a rambling, meaningless "pooling of ignorance."

3. In Discussion, some students may never participate while a few may tend to dominate, which necessitates the teaching of collaborative skills that create a sense of psychological safety

such that students feel their ideas and comments will be listened to by classmates.

4. Long and/or frequent periods of silence can occur in a Discussion. Such silence often leads the teacher to take over the class in pursuit of the topic.

5. Whether or not the class members will get into a Discussion on the topic is always a risk.

6. It is possible that a topic will be such that the students get carried away. They might get too emotionally involved, and matters may get out of hand.

7. Teachers often become frustrated because Discussion may fail to lead to a conclusion, or at least to the conclusion the teacher believes to be most desirable.

8. Students often lack the informational background or maturity to contribute to a meaningful Discussion.

9. Finally, there is the problem of evaluation. How does one accurately measure the contribution of a given student to the Discussion?

Guidelines for Maximum Utilization

1. An atmosphere of "acceptance" must exist in the classroom. If the classroom atmosphere has in the past been one of hostility and strain between the teacher and students, Discussion will not work. Students must feel free from threat in order to speak openly.

2. The teacher must be prepared. The teacher must be familiar with the content to be considered, the characteristics of the group activity, and the materials and resources available to the students.

3. The students must be prepared. In order to ensure that the Discussion reaches a level higher than a "sharing of ignorance," the teacher must plan sufficient learning activities prior to the Discussion.

4. Discussion should be used when teacher objectives are considered worth the extra time required. Generally, the objectives appropriate to the Discussion process would involve higher-level cognitive, affective, and skill learning related to Discussion.

5. The topics for Discussion should be properly stated. Primarily, the topic should be stated as an issue to "polarize" viewpoints. Secondly, the words used to phrase the issue should be terms familiar to the students. Finally, the topic itself should be one which has some degree of personal relevance for the students.

6. In introducing the subject matter to be discussed, the question or issue should be presented in very specifically defined terms to the students. Writing the topic on the board or in hand-out material is well worth the effort.

7. When introducing the topic, take time to clarify terms, establish the relevance of the topic, and create a sense of psychological safety in the classroom

8. Use panels, forums, debates, or buzz-sessions on occasion to lead up to whole-class Discussion. These take time to organize and plan, but the variety can help motivate, and there is the assurance that at least a few students will be prepared.

9. The teacher serves as moderator of the Discussion while it is in progress. The moderator clarifies concepts, makes tentative summaries, states conclusions, and keeps the Discussion on track.

10. Respect silence and the contribution it can make. Learn to discern the nature of the silence. If the silence is due to the

fact that students are thinking, they should be allowed to think. If the silence is due to confusion, clarify the last question or summarize the Discussion up to that point.

11. Encourage many students to participate, but do so unceremoniously. A question directed to a specific student or a simple "What do you think, John?" will suffice. Realize that not every student will need to have something to say on every topic. Be satisfied that several students may discuss any given topic, and that all participated over several topics at one time or another.

12. Discourage dominance of a few by handling the situation privately. Merely inform the overly eager students that you appreciate their efforts and want them to continue, but that others need to be heard from too. If this does not do it, a little more direct statement needs to be made in private.

13. Always have a summary when the Discussion is over. This may be done by the teacher, but is better if done by the students. The Discussion has been in vain if the students are unaware of the conclusions reached, positions taken on the issue, or processes undergone.

14. Look for related activities. Successful Discussion will lead naturally into follow-up activities which will enhance the student's learning.

15. Unless specified as a designed objective, student Discussion should not be evaluated for grading purposes. This is the only way to encourage students to contribute freely and honestly to the Discussion. To use participation in the Discussion as a factor in grading only encourages the student to "psych-out" the teacher and then provide the desired answer.

Summary

Discussion is a most important strategy on a number of levels. First, it involves the coverage of academics. Secondly, it involves a sharing of ideas *between students*, rather than an osmotic process from teacher to student. Thirdly, it is a schooling in social interaction, courtesy, leadership/followership, thought organization, and conversation. In this last level is the preparation for students to become proficient speakers/listeners and worthwhile contributing citizens - a goal found in every school philosophy.

Discussion does demand supervision and guidance by the teacher. One well-known killer of effective Discussion is "rambling" or "loss-of-target" talking. This is a sure sign of boredom or lack of direction and calls for teacher intervention in an appropriate manner. The lack-of-knowledge problem which results in ineffective Discussion demands that the teacher be prepared to point out bolstering relevant resources prior to the Discussion if possible.

Questions to Promote Discussion

1. From your experiences, is Discussion a worthwhile strategy to use? Why or why not?

2. Why is it essential for the teacher to think about Discussion in terms of both "content" and "process?"

3. What do you think is the major reason so many Discussions turn out to be unproductive?

4. What are the most important guidelines which should be used to ensure a productive Discussion? Why?

DRILL

Definition and Description

Although there are many sub-types, Drill is a teaching technique intended to bring about automatic accuracy and speed of performance in any subject. The aim of Drill, then is the fixation of correct information or skill through repetition.

Some use the term "drill" only for mental ideas and the term "practice" for motor activity. However, since both are based on repetition, "drill" and "practice" will be used here synonymously.

Advantages or Special Purposes

1. Drill is especially applicable in kinesthetic (skill) and low-level cognitive learning.

2. Some knowledge cannot be retained by a single exposure, thus requiring Drill (e.g., multiplication tables).

3. In skill development, repetitious practice is essential to build competence and technique mastery.

4. Students can build their own associations of information through Drill.

5. Used in student tutorial situations, it can be a means of creating motivation.

6. Slower students can be used as tutors.

7. Affective learning can take place by grouping the slow and fast achievers as a Drill team.

8. Drill can be used in time allotments of short duration when no other activities are planned.

Disadvantages or Limitations

1. Drill can become boring and monotonous.

2. Information acquired through Drill will not be retained long without use.

3. Overuse of Drill can lead students (*and* teachers) to believe in memorization as an end.

4. Drill reduces learning to a purely mechanical act.

Guidelines for maximum Utilization

1. Use Drill only when automatic speed and accuracy or performance learning is the objective.

2. Make sure students understand the purpose of the Drill or practice.

3. Use both individual and group "concert" exercises.

4. Use games and contests to add interest to Drill.

5. Make sure students are practicing with correct information or processes. It is only *correct* practice which makes perfect.

6. Organize Drill periods with regard to proper spacing and length of Drill time. Over-practice produces boredom and fatigue.

7. Provide the opportunity for students to apply that which is mastered through Drill.

Summary

The function of Drill is solely to create automatic responses to specific stimuli. If you were effectively drilled in multiplication and someone came up behind you and said quickly, "What's 9 X 9?" Your response should be "81," instantly, without thinking about it. Football drills in throwing an effective block are designed to teach the player to do it automatically. Instruction in memorizing the capitals of the United States is another example. It is a practice closely paralleled by programming a computer. The teacher should remember that this is the only purpose of Drill. It has nothing to do with elevating mental functioning or making better citizens. Overused, Drill is a surefire method of dulling cognitive abilities and promoting discipline problems. The percentage of class time spent on Drill exercises should be minimal.

Questions to Promote Discussion

1. Is the statement "Practice makes perfect" a true one? Why or why not?

2. Does Drill belong in the teacher's kit of strategies? Why or why not?

3. Explain the chief disadvantages of Drill.

4. What is the most important guideline for the successful use of Drill? Why?

5. In what areas of your curriculum might drill be most appropriate? Why?

FIELD STUDY (TRIPS)

Definition and Description

According to *The Dictionary of Education,* Field Study is, "a trip arranged by the school and undertaken for educational purposes, in which students go to places where the materials of instruction may be observed and studied directly in their functional settings."

A sub-function of the *community resources* strategy, Field Studies are generally made to points of instructional interest such as factories, public utilities, museums, libraries, art galleries, or government installations. They may also include scientific forays to streams, ponds, fields and forests, to collect specimens for immediate or future studies.

Advantages or Special Purposes

1. Field Studies provide the student with interesting, first-hand experiences.

2. A common experience is provided for students which can serve as a basis for other learning activities.

3. Students become more aware of their environment.

4. Field Studies can add greatly to school-community relationships.

5. What is learned can have great impact due to the multi-sensory nature of the experience.

6. Field Study can be utilized by teachers of any and all subject areas in the curriculum.

7. Field Studies extend classroom learning through reality.

8.   Field Trips are a change of pace from the usual classroom activities.

Disadvantages or Limitations

1.   The legal responsibilities accompanying a Field Study are serious.

2.   Discipline can easily become a problem.

3.   Administrative procedures to organize Field Trips are often so complicated that they discourage taking them.

4.   Transportation arrangements are often difficult or costly.

5.   When a teacher has students for only one period a day it is difficult to make arrangements which do not create conflicts with other classes.

6.   Field Trips require additional chaperons and these may be difficult to secure.

7.   If not properly planned the Field Study becomes a waste of time and takes away from valuable learning activities.

8.   An improperly planned trip may deter other teachers and place doubt in the mind of the administration about the value of this strategy.

Guidelines for Maximum Utilization

1.   Before even considering the Field Trip, become familiar with the legal aspects of teacher liability involved.

2.   Make sure the Field Trip is of educational value in that it relates directly to what is being taught in the classroom.

3. Plan the Field Trip by visiting the site and talking with the people before actually making the decision to undertake the Field Study.

4. Obtain permission from school authorities.

5. Make all transportation arrangements.

6. Notify parents to obtain consent. Parents often like to go along giving added supervision as well as driving help.

7. Prepare the class by relating the trip to what is being studied and what they might observe.

8. Establish safety, dress and behavior standards.

9. At the site, provide for adequate supervision.

10. Be sure all students are where they are supposed to be.

11. Handle small incidents as they occur. Do not let unsafe behavior continue.

12. Upon return to the classroom, review and summarize what was learned on the Field Trip.

13. Have the class send a "thank you" message to the hosts of the Field Trip.

14. Develop a means for evaluating pupils and the place visited in order to assist in planning future trips.

Summary

One of the long-standing major criticisms of education has been its sponsorship of cloistered, unrealistic learning of irrelevant facts. Field Study is one means of overcoming this criticism. It provides opportunity for students to see the "real world" in action, and, thereby, widens their attitudinal, social, and academic horizons.

Careful planning and pre-visitation to the site by the teacher is essential if the experience is to be useful and valuable to students. Undoubtedly, thousands of field trips have been a wasted, futile experience because of insufficient pre-planning. Students should receive some definite "coaching" in observation skills and an outline of objectives and purposes prior to the Field Trip. Follow-up activities including discussion, writing short essays, drawing pictures, or model-making will ensure that retention of the objectives is accomplished.

Field Study, properly carried out, can be a major source of enrichment for learners.

Questions to Promote Discussion

1. What do you consider the major value of a Field Trip? Why?

2. What do you consider the chief drawback of the Field Trip? Why?

3. Do you feel the answer to Question #1 outweighs the answer to Question #2, or vice versa? Why?

4. What would you do if, at the last moment, the parents of a student in your class refused to let their child participate in a planned field trip? Is your suggested solution fair to all involved?

5. Does a waiver signed by a parent prevent the school from being sued by that family if their child is injured on the trip?

FUTURISTIC FORECASTING

Definition and Description

Futuristics is the process of projecting into the future and attempting to forecast what noteworthy events will take place; what the world and its people will be like; where our food, clothing and housing will come from; how society in general may function to maintain a safe and peaceful world, etc.

As an example, a student or group of students may undertake the problem of transportation. What form will it take? With the present pollution problems, what form of fuel will be used to eliminate pollution and its ill effects on society? What effect will the movement of the population to the outlying areas of large cities have on the choice of transportation? These and many more areas could be included in the study of this type of problem under the heading of Futuristic Forecasting.

This strategy, properly used, requires a combination of skills. *Research, field trips, community resources* and *individualized study* permit the student to be creative in a useful way.

Futuristic Forecasting is a form of directed daydreaming. It requires supportive data, logical thinking, statistical study and good analytical skills. It is a strategy that can be used in almost any subject area and yet it supports and enforces the basic skills of reading, writing and mathematics. (See *simulation* also.)

Advantages or Special Purposes

1. It is an opportunity to study socialization in such a way as to make individuals question the status quo.

2. It permits continuous change and frequent modification and/or abandonment of courses and units of learning experiences.

3. Futuristic forecasting is, or can be, an individualized learning tool.

4. It is an opportunity for students to specialize in an area of their choice.

5. Futuristics helps to prepare students to become researchers, developers, disseminators and/or practitioners.

6. It provides students an intensive choice in the selection of one area to intellectually challenge their interests.

7. It expands the school learning environment by requiring the use of facilities outside the classroom and/or building.

8. The opportunity to use a wide range of resource persons and consultants is made possible in this strategy.

Disadvantages or Limitations

1. All studies and changes are based on the assumption of uncertainty.

2. Teachers may fear to delve into the area of the unknown.

3. The school administration may frown on teachers leaving the approved curriculum to study the unknown.

4. Technological facilities may not be available (either in the school or in the nearby community) to carry studies far enough into the future to be of worthwhile value.

5. Students who have been programmed in the traditional ways of learning may not be cognatively sophisticated enough to pursue the unknown.

6.   If very little information is available to conduct a study of the future the student will lose interest.

Guidelines for Maximum Utilization

1.   Enter this strategy with caution and with a short-term project in the beginning.

2.   Ensure a complete understanding and acceptance by all parties concerned (school administration, parents and pupils) prior to beginning studies in Futuristics.

3.   Develop a clear set of objectives for yourself and have the students do likewise at the outset of a Futuristic study.

4.   Once the process is begun, allow the students to think creatively even to extremes.

5.   Attempt to foresee what resources will be needed and if they are available locally.

6.   Direct student projects and studies into categories useful to mankind, i.e., food production needs, mobility of society, transportation requirements of mass populations, land use, etc.

7.   Keep an open mind. Do not attempt to limit students' thinking, as the projected changes are based on assumptions of uncertainty.

8.   Guide and direct the pupils, but don't dictate.

Summary

Who knows at this time what the future holds in store for humankind? With the advances of science and technology, there is much room for uncertainty.

This strategy offers the opportunity for students and teachers to dream, to think, and to play games regarding what they believe the world will be like in the year 2050 and beyond. It allows the opportunity to forecast without being hurt or penalized for making wrong forecasts or conclusions. It is a form of *simulation gaming*.

Certainly there were many people at the time who had not dreamed that Neil Armstrong or anyone else would walk on the moon. Why not allow students to forecast what they see in the future and attempt to support their theories? This strategy will expand their creative thinking, their research skills and their ability to find support for their beliefs. It is a combination of strategies including *research, demonstration, individualized instruction, field study, community resources* and many others. What the students forecast now may in actuality come true in their lifetime.

Questions to Promote Discussion

1. What subject areas seem most suited to Futuristic Forecasting? How?

2. How would you structure a forecasting session, i.e., introduction, guidelines, rules, resources, summary?

3. Resources are important to the success of Futuristic Forecasting. List all the potential resources you could have access to in your particular situation.

INDEPENDENT STUDY

Definition and Description

Independent Study is an arrangement whereby the student explores in-depth an area of interest not normally studied by the entire class. At the post-secondary level, Independent Study is often used when there is a conflict in schedules or to cover a required subject not presently being offered. The topic to be explored can be assigned by the teacher or selected by the student with the teacher's approval. The aim is to provide a unique learning experience for the student. (See *student research, project,* and *laboratory.*)

Advantages or Special Purposes

1. Individual students can work in an area of need. For example, brighter students can extend their learning while slower students can focus on an area of deficiency.

2. Students are more motivated when they are studying something they have selected and in which they have a special interest.

3. Learning can be truly individualized, breaking the "lockstep" atmosphere of schools.

4. Individual students assume more responsibility for learning and the presenting of their projects or reports helps other students to gain new insights into the study topic.

5. Students gain insights into "how" to learn.

6. Independent Study fosters self-teaching skills and attitudes.

7. All subject areas may be encompassed in this strategy.

8. A variety of exhibits can be used to demonstrate the results of a student's independent efforts.

Disadvantages or Limitations

1. The flexible schedules necessary to permit students and teachers to do true Independent Study may be lacking.

2. A shortage of related materials or other resources necessary to carry out the study may restrict independent work.

3. A lack of research skills on the part of the student and teacher may hinder completion of the project strategy.

4. Without proper background skills and training, a lack of initiative may become a severe problem in bringing the Independent Study project to a final conclusion.

5. The teacher must maintain a constant check of student progress where Independent Study programs are in operation.

6. Large amounts of time may be required of the teacher to help each student individualize a program.

7. Evaluation is more challenging.

Guidelines for Maximum Utilization

1. Do not permit too many students to work on the same type of project. Often one student will do the major portion of the work and all will receive the same amount of credit in the final evaluation.

2. Take sufficient time at the beginning to help each student clarify the area of study. The student must have a clear understanding of the direction and limits of the study to be undertaken. Clearly specified objectives should be stated at the outset of the project.

3.   Determine the availability of resources before beginning this strategy.

4.   Allow sufficient time to complete the project, but do not allow the project to continue endlessly (deadlines are usually beneficial).

5.   Do not permit students to embark on studies which are not appropriate to class instruction. Students may be permitted to suggest areas of study, but you must have final approval to ensure the appropriateness of the study.

6.   It may be necessary to check progress at periodic intervals to review the individual's efforts and to provide additional guidance toward culmination of the project.

7.   Determine in advance how the project will be presented for final evaluation. Criteria to determine the value of the project or the final grade evaluation should be established prior to the approval of an Independent Study proposal.

8.   Permitting the students to share the results of their study with the rest of the class can add a dimension to the activity.

9.   Make arrangements for alternate activities for those students who finish their project(s) earlier than anticipated.

Example

Hal Lockett, a high school history teacher, was having difficulty motivating one of his students in world history. In his evening graduate course in educational psychology he broached the subject to the professor, Dr. Whizz, a local school psychologist and adjunct instructor at the university.

"So," Dr. Whizz began, "you've tried the praise, the threats, the *let me be your friend* approaches, and nothing happened?"

"No," Harold replied, "he just slumps in his seat, scowls, and mutters, *What good is this stuff anyway?*"

"What does interest him?" Whizz queried.

"I don't know," Hal responded, "unless it's automobiles. He's always drawing cars, or reading auto magazines or shooting the bull with a guy next to him about engines, tune-ups, or racing slicks."

Dr. Whizz paced the front of the room for a few seconds. He suddenly stopped and looked straight at Hal. "Hal, what's going to happen to this fellow if you can't get him motivated in history?"

"Why, he'll get an F the way he's going."

"Exactly," exclaimed Whizz, "and that's why you have nothing to lose by catering to his interest, do you?"

Startled, Hal sat up straight. "What do you mean?"

"Look, Hal, do you really care how the boy learns history? I mean does he have to learn it your way or not at all?"

"Why, I don't care. I'd just be tickled to see him getting interested in the course. He's really got too much potential to flunk out of school."

"Good," the instructor responded, "so why not let him learn his world history by following the history of transportation from ancient times up to the modern automobile?"

"But," Hal questioned, "what about the curriculum guide? It doesn't allow for such an approach."

Dr. Whizz removed his glasses, his eyes glowing with intensity. "Hal, you and the curriculum guide are in existence to serve the learner, but curriculum guides are constructed to serve the majority of students. They will never meet the needs of every student. The teacher must maintain discretionary freedom in utilizing such guides---tailoring them to suit particular differences in students, whether those differences be class-wide or individual. You are hired to teach history successfully. If you pursue this student with the curriculum guide he will fail, and so will you. If you feel insecure, go to your principal and explain why and how you wish to set up an independent study with this boy. I'm sure he will buy the ideas."

"OK," Hal responded, "how do I go about setting up an independent study?"

"First of all you locate the resources necessary for the project. Check libraries (by phone to save time), including school, public, and county libraries. Check not only for books, but also magazine articles, films, filmstrips, pamphlets, and reference works. This ensures that the necessary resources are available. This is all done prior to springing the idea on the student. When you present him with the new approach, you want to know in advance what kind of structure you wish him to follow. Now this doesn't mean he cannot have input into the particular areas of concentration---encourage it---but *you* are the teacher. You establish the structure. This means you set the deadlines, and types of reporting (book reports, readings, projects, oral reports, etc.), record-keeping, and evaluation schema. It is very important that before he begins, the student be fully aware of:

1.   The objectives you specifically wish him to accomplish;

2.   How you wish him to go about fulfilling the objectives, i.e., book reports, term papers, projects, etc.; and,

3.   How he will be evaluated.

"The other crucial factor is that you touch base with him *every day* as to his progress. At least ask him, *How is it going?* or something to that effect. *And*, at least once a week, check the folder and/or physical evidence of progress. Praise, encourage, cajole him until he gets in the swing of things. What do you think, will it work?"

"Yes, it certainly seems worth trying. Transportation history should catch his interest if anything will."

"Well," Dr. Whizz smiled, "it should provide a good vehicle for motivating him."

The class groaned.

Summary

Independent Study requires the teacher to allow the student to become the teacher. The teacher becomes a guide-on-the-side. The teacher is a facilitator rather than a lecturer, an encourager rather than a demander, and a clarifier rather than a seeing-eye dog. It is not a time for rest and relaxation. If anything, the teacher must be more vigilant and more available for help than ever. Constant assessment of progress, conferring with the learner and viewing his/her work, is extremely important. Independent study asks for an exhibition of concern---the greatest motivator one human can offer another.

Questions to Promote Discussion

1. The authors of this book feel the biggest weakness of our schools is not preparing students to learn "how" to learn. Do you agree or not? Why?

2. What do you consider to be the major limitation to using Independent Study in the classroom? What do you recommend to overcome that limitation?

3. What specific skills and attitudes do you think a student might develop through Independent Study that would not be learned in a "lockstep" classroom?

4. In using the Independent Study strategy, the teacher functions in a non-traditional manner. What are some teacher behaviors which must be adopted to use Independent Study? Would you be comfortable with those behaviors? Why or why not?

INDIVIDUALIZED LEARNING

Definition and Description

Individualized Learning is a broad, almost philosophical approach to the teaching-learning process. It involves an assessment of student needs and interests, a tailoring of subject matter and teaching strategies to meet those needs and interests, and constant monitoring and guidance of student progress. A teacher using this approach would employ a number of strategies; the concept of Individualized Learning is too universal to be applicable as a specific strategy. This universality is one of the reasons why the approach is not as widespread as most people believe it should be. In this amorphous state it is as difficult to understand as the concepts of patriotism, truth, and brotherly love. As with these concepts, Individualized Learning is understandable only through its displayed components: resources such as *learning packets, independent study, contracting, student research, programmed instruction, interest centers, interview, projects, Socratic, case study* and *student tutorial* strategies.

Advantages or Special Purposes

1. Each student moves at his own pace through a level of subject matter (matched with assessed abilities), using a teaching/ learning strategy selected to promote optimal progress.

2. Students are not floundering in material beyond their grasp or bored by material too easy for them.

3. Students are not penalized for being out of school for illness or family matters. Upon return each student can pick up at the point where he/she was temporarily halted.

4. Students are not in false competition with peers. They are only in competition with themselves.

5. Retention of learning is improved (over non-individualized instruction).

6. The instructor is truly a facilitating teacher wisely selecting a learning program to meet an individual's needs. The teacher observes daily activity and assists and/or adjusts programs as required.

7. The teacher has more opportunity to pinpoint and assist in solving individual student problems.

8. Many discipline problems arising from boredom and frustration are eliminated.

9. Evaluation takes the form of reporting actual individual accomplishments rather than the nebulous ABCDF grading system.

10. Students learn to take more responsibility for their own instructional activities.

11. Students have the opportunity to see their personal progress and tend to extend their knowledge rather than stopping at minimal levels of accomplishment.

Disadvantages or Limitations

1. Time and effort must be expended in developing materials and matching strategies to a given student.

2. Pre-assessment of student academic status takes time and special skill.

3. Students must be taught to handle Individualized Learning situations---a time-consuming activity.

4. Record-keeping can be lengthy and involved. (See *portfolios.)*

5. In the beginning, Individualized Learning takes more teacher monitoring time.

6. Parents and administrators may be disturbed by the absence of letter grades.

7. The classroom physical structure and the classroom furniture may be limiting.

8. There is more movement and "noise" in an individualized classroom.

9. Appropriate resource materials may simply be unavailable.

10. Students may tend to work in competition with classmates rather than accept the challenge of self-improvement.

11. The teacher must be prepared to initiate new and continuing projects and study topics for those who learn and/or complete their work in shorter periods of time.

Guidelines for Maximum Utilization

Guidelines under each component strategy required should be consulted for specifics, but a few general helpful hints are in order.

1. Be prepared to gradually direct students away from the traditional to the individualized classroom. This will entail a great deal of structure at first until students become self-motivating and responsible.

2. Parents and pertinent administrators should be consulted for approval and kept informed prior to and during the program.

3. Careful records of individual accomplishments need to be kept, noting each student's daily progress.

4. Pre-assessment is an integral part of Individualized Learning. Different methods are plentiful, depending on the types of information required:

A. If physical health information is needed, consider the school nurse, cumulative records, parents, dialogue with the student, and your own observations.

B. If special learning disability information is needed you can rely on diagnostic tests, medical records, and conferences with the doctor, school psychologist, and parents.

C. To discover student interests and needs, use interest inventories, straightforward communication with the students, parent conferences and observation.

D. To learn about specific subject matter abilities, the use of pretests, conferences with the student's former teachers, achievement records, and observation will provide valuable information. Different subject matter may require different means of assessment.

5. Objectives should be clearly stated on paper and understood by the student.

6. Objectives and the time, material, and procedures necessary to achieve them should vary with each student's interest and capabilities.

7. Students should have some voice in selecting their objectives, materials, procedures, and time-span for completion. Ideally, they may eventually develop their own objectives and procedures.

8. Teacher and student must know at the outset what factors will be used for evaluation of the lesson material. A variety of evaluation techniques may be necessary in order to assure that each student is evaluated on his/her performance. Examples include: the quality of the work; grammatical quality; the number of biographical entries used; the ability of the student

undertaking the individualized work; and the methods of presentation of learning results.

Summary

The processes used in Individualized Learning are not new. The good teacher has been aware of and has used them on a regular basis--- but they have been directed at the entire class. Thus, the strategy has not been exploited to its fullest potential.

Although the strategy is time consuming at the outset, the rewards tend to far exceed the energy expended. Students involved in individualized programs are encouraged to exceed minimal standards. They are further prompted to expand on lessons assigned to areas of their personal and intellectual interests. Consequently, learning becomes an exciting adventure and not a necessary obligation to complete the same daily activities that are performed in the typical classroom. It is truly a challenge to the intellectually inclined student but does not penalize those students who need to maintain a slower pace to accomplish the minimal requirements.

When coupled with other strategies such as *interest centers, student research*, and independent *laboratory* experiences, a program in Individualized Learning is a challenge to the student and a blessing to the busy teacher.

Questions to Promote Discussion

1. Should Individualized Learning be listed as a separate strategy in a book on teaching strategies? Why or why not?

2. What is the major advantage of Individualized Learning?

3. What is the major disadvantage of Individualized Learning?

4. Which carries more weight, the advantage noted in response to Question #2 or the disadvantage noted in answer to Question #3? Why?

INQUIRY

Definition and Description

The Inquiry method is used to train students in the use of scientific methods to develop causal reasoning processes. Students begin by describing a phenomena they have witnessed. They then use Inquiry to investigate and explain the event. They develop concepts, test hypotheses and provide alternative solutions.

Students are naturally curious and Inquiry training provides a conduit for acquiring and organizing information, processing data in a manner that models scholarly models of logical reasoning. The model also reveals to students the tentative nature of theories and explanations. Through the group process students also recognize the value of alternative ideas and solutions.

Advantages and Special Purposes

1. Students' natural curiosity provides energy and excitement for learner motivation.

2. Students become conscious of their questions and need for answers.

3. Students learn to analyze thinking strategies.

4. New thinking strategies can be added.

5. Inquiry models provide excellent opportunities for *cooperative learning* exercises.

6. Students learn the phases of scientific reasoning through active learning.

7. The Inquiry method can be used with students of all ages.

Disadvantages or Limitations

1. Teacher role can become too dominating and inhibit students' active involvement.

2. Aggressive children may end up dominating the experience.

3. The teacher may tend to emphasize the infallibility of logic rather than identifying its tentative nature.

Guidelines for Utilization

1. Students' questions should require yes or no responses.

2. Invalid questions should be rephrased by students until a "yes" or "no" can be given as a response.

3. Point out erroneous assumptions being made by the students.

4. Use the language of scientific Inquiry.

5. Remain non-judgmental using the brainstorming strategy by not evaluating student theory.

6. Encourage continued clarification of student thinking.

7. Require support for generalizations made by students.

8. Facilitate interaction among all students.

Summary

Inquiry begins by explaining the procedures to be used in scientific reasoning. Students examine an event, gather data and verify various aspects of the scenario. They isolate variables, develop hypotheses and test causal relationships. They then formulate rules and explanations, analyze the inquiry process itself and seek to develop more effective strategies for delving and explaining.

Questions to Promote Discussion

1. Why does the author suggest that teachers need to emphasize the tentative nature of scientific reasoning?

2. What reasonable responses could a teacher make to a parent who complains that this process creates problems at home because the child is now questioning her parents?

3. How could TESA (Teacher Expectation and Student Achievement) strategies be incorporated to insure that inquiry lessons are not dominated by aggressive students.

4. How could the *cooperative learning* model facilitate an Inquiry lesson?

INTEREST (LEARNING) CENTERS

Definition and Description

Establishing an Interest Centered Classroom (ICC) involves actual division of the physical space into stations of various academic areas. In an elementary classroom, for example, one might have a science center, a language arts center, a math center, a social science center, an art center, etc. An upper elementary or secondary classroom in biology might have a genetics center, a bacteriology center, an ecology center, an anatomy center, etc. Located in each center are abundant materials and equipment pertaining to that particular center's purpose.

In the "pure form" interest center, students spend as much time as they wish in any center. Variations are common in this strategy. Some teachers "contract" (see *contracting*) with students for objectives and time spent in each center, or require a certain amount of time per week in each interest center, or require a project in each interest center, etc.

Advantages or Special Purposes

1. Interest Centers provide for individualized learning within constraints of subject matter requirements.

2. Interest Centers allow students to devote more time to the subjects which interest them personally.

3. The teacher is free to move about from center to center assisting students.

4. Students have the opportunity to bring in their own materials with which to work.

5. *Community resource* people in each interest area can be brought in easily to work with a small group of students.

6. Students are more responsible for their own learning activities.

7. The use of student tutors may work well in this strategy.

8. Where physical constraints limit the number of centers, a singl‹ center can be designated for a topical study and changed late› to meet the next area or unit of study.

Disadvantages or Limitations

1. The physical arrangement of effective Interest Centers almos necessitates the replacement of individual student desks witl tables and chairs and/or carpeting.

2. The need for varied materials in each center may be constraint.

3. A great deal of preparation of environment, materials, an‹ students is required.

4. Record-keeping of student achievement can be difficult.

5. Students may be lacking in self-motivation---especially if the have not had prior independent work.

6. The teacher needs a good command of all subject matter.

7. The self-motivating, interest-based student behavior may nc thrill administrators and parents as much as it does the student: Students make "noise" and move about more in an interest centered class.

8. If students leave an interest-based class/year for a non-interest based class/year there may be a problem with their re adjustment.

Guidelines for Maximum Utilization

1. You must secure an abundance of materials and some equipment pertinent to each center well in advance of the beginning of the year. This involves a lot of time, and some begging or borrowing from local businesses, individuals, hospitals, etc. (unless you have no budget problems). The type and quantity of materials depend on the objectives for each center. It is amazing how much you can gain by donation if you just ask.

2. Resource people are a valuable asset to an interest-based classroom. Likewise, they must be lined up and informed as to what is expected of them ahead of time. Often it is possible to have a resource person come in regularly to work with a small group in a certain field. Just as with materials, it is amazing how many experts are pleased to donate their time and energy to work with students. Do not fail to utilize some students' parents and acquaintances as valuable resources.

3. Administration and parents should be kept informed and/or consulted during the planning and program operation.

4. If students are not acquainted with self-motivating classrooms, it will be essential to have a "weaning period" during which they are structured into their activities (perhaps by *contracting*) rather closely at first. As individual students gain more confidence and responsibility they can begin structuring their own learning activities.

5. Each student should have a folder kept in a central file where he or she logs his activities and achievements. If contracts are utilized, they should also be kept in the folder for both your and the students' referral. Care should be taken that accurate and detailed records are kept; otherwise, assessment becomes impossible.

6. Another possibility for assessment is to require each student to exhibit some level of individual proficiency on small quizzes or written exercises.

7. Depending on how structured the situation is, students can be encouraged to bring their own materials and *community resources* after being cleared by the teacher.

8. Many other strategies can operate effectively within the interest-centered classroom---*projects, independent study, research, student tutorial, field trips, learning packets,* etc.   As an example, the *behavior modification* strategy can be utilized by setting up an Interest Center of games. Students can go there for free time after completing a specified amount of academic work.

Summary

Interest Center teaching can be a terrific blessing. It individualizes learning, makes students more responsible for their own time (allows them to spend more time where needed), encourages communication with the "outside world," and eliminates many motivational problems. It also makes progress reporting easier and meaningful, as parents can be shown the student's portfolio on what he/she has actually accomplished rather than a letter grade.

A major objection to this type of classroom operation is the procurement of materials and equipment; this is, in actuality, a display of non-initiative and non-imagination on the part of the objector. A good creative teacher can procure almost anything for little or no cost (a rocket was acquired by one teacher!) if proper communication is established. Federal, state and local agencies have literally tons of material and equipment that can be donated or at least borrowed. Many agencies, such as the State Department of Natural Resources, large industry, law enforcement, etc., have people on their staff whose main function is to perform public relations work. There is a wealth of knowledge and skill in one of our most ignored resources---the retired professional.

Hospital personnel, veterinarians and engineers are usually very willing to visit classrooms. The list goes on and on.

With proper introduction and monitoring the teacher may find that Interest-Centered teaching provides the valuable organizational assistance for which he or she has been searching.

Questions to Promote Discussion

1. Would you expect the students at the grade level which you anticipate teaching to be in favor of using Interest Centers? Why or why not?

2. Assuming you had the materials and space, what do you think the major obstacle to using Interest Centers would be? Why?

3. What steps could you take to overcome this obstacle?

4. What would you predict to be the "future" of the use of Interest Centers? Why?

INTERVIEW

Definition and Description

The interview is basically a data-gathering technique using pre planned questions to determine the feelings and attitudes of an individual a specific group, the school, or the community on an issue of hig interest. It is closely related to the survey in that both seek to develo data---one by oral questioning and the other through written response.

The Interview is especially helpful in practicing a one-on-on situation such as a guidance counselor-student Interview or a student citizen Interview on a pre-established question or problem. It may b used in random sampling of a few people to establish a trend (similar t Gallup or Harris Polls) or in seeking opinions from high public official and other select individuals.

An Interview is performed in a systematic fashion within a fev simple guidelines:

1. Outline the general plan.

2. Establish rapport with the respondent.

3. State the issue, question or problem.

4. Elicit a response to the issue, question or problem.

5. Record the data.

6. Close the Interview.

7. Evaluate and report findings.

Advantages or Special Purposes

1. Interviews encourage students to plan and think in a systematic fashion.

2. This is an excellent method for collecting data from individuals and groups.

3. It is especially useful in collection of information related to community attitudes and personal opinions.

4. Persons interviewed generally have a high degree of interest and a desire to express their personal opinion.

5. Through the use of this strategy, information on an issue or problem can be collected quickly.

6. Interviewing helps develop rapport between the school and the community.

7. It can be used as an individual or total class project.

8. If well planned, it helps bring the pupil face-to-face with community realities.

Disadvantages or Limitations

1. The teacher must spend a substantial amount of time helping students develop questioning techniques.

2. Interviewing requires a coordinated effort of all involved, and this can disrupt school or administrative routines.

3. A poorly planned Interview can result in erroneous learning and impaired public relations.

4. Students tend to take sides on an issue rather than remain neutral.

5. Data gathered may be difficult to interpret and report.

6. The class may not be of sufficient maturity to face the obligations required in performing Interviews, especially when meeting older members of the community.

7. Interviews tend to elicit personal opinions and may not be factual or usable in the final reports.

Guidelines for Maximum Utilization

1. Plan Interviews well in advance and rehearse techniques prior to actual Interview situations.

2. Be selective in choosing questions and issues. The issue should be relevant and interesting, the questions clear and designed to gather the necessary type and amount of data.

3. Develop specific questions. (Note: the teacher may want to review the strategy of *questioning* at this point.)

4. The questions should be free of bias.

5. Before initiating this strategy, secure administrative approval.

6. Students should avoid taking sides on an issue (until all data are in and analyzed).

7. Encourage students to be pleasant, courteous and tactful during Interviews.

8. During the Interview take notes in brief written form, or, if using a recorder, secure permission in advance to record the remarks.

9. Establish guidelines with which to evaluate results prior to actual Interviews.

10. Be prepared to respond to the subject's return questions.

Summary

Crucial to the success of the Interview strategy is preparation in: (1) knowing the background of the subject; (2) knowing the information desired from the Interview; and, (3) knowing what questions need to be asked to accumulate that information.

An important facet of interviewing is the attitude of the person conducting the Interview. A successful interviewer rivets his/her attention to the person being interviewed, as if the rest of the world has disappeared. That person is the most important in the world---his/her words are pearls of wisdom, drops of pure nectar, and if not attended to will be lost forever. (In actuality, this may be more truth than poetry, and not a bad attitude for students to develop.) The interviewer, in effect, creates a vacuum (a dismissal of his own identity) which draws out information from the subject.

Interview is a useful strategy. It teaches students to gather information in a logical and respectful fashion from a most valuable temporary resource---another human being. This has been the basis of recent usage to document "living history" lessons.

Questions to Promote Discussion

1. Name a project in which students could serve as interviewers.

2. What would be the major advantage for students conducting Interviews in this subject?

3. Why is student interviewing not often used by teachers?

LABORATORY

Definition and Description

The *Dictionary of Education* defines the Laboratory strategy as:

the instructional procedure by which the cause, effect, nature or property of any phenomenon, whether social, psychological or physical is determined by actual experience or experiment under controlled conditions.

In its "pure" form, Laboratory was conceived to be a sterile, well equipped room with white-coated technicians carrying out a variety of experiments and activities. Today, Laboratory is defined as the place where an individual or group study some phenomenon, subject, lesson, etc. It could be a reading lab, outdoor education center, science facility, or an ordinary classroom.

In simple terms, Laboratory is a supervised learning activity carried out by the student studying a particular subject involving practical application of theory through observation, experimentation, and research.

Advantages or Special Purposes

1. Students can capitalize on their own interests.

2. The teacher is free to offer individual assistance and instruction to those students needing special attention.

3. The activity may be carried out by individual students or in small groups.

4. Instruction may be done through the use of self-instructional materials, devices or machines.

5. Laboratory is basically a problem-solving technique, usually of short duration.

6. This strategy helps students learn to generalize and to apply generalizations in new situations.

7. As a learning activity, it reinforces the *discovery* and *inquiry* approaches to learning.

8. Laboratory simulates actual scientific experiments including the formulation of hypotheses, testing the hypotheses, recording and reporting the findings.

9. Students increase their ability to do the tasks more effectively, more skillfully, and more independently.

10. It is an excellent motivational strategy.

11. Groups are provided the opportunity to share in the results and findings of individual projects.

Disadvantages or Limitations

1. The approved projects must be within the range of the students' abilities.

2. The maturity of the students may be insufficient to pursue long-range goals established.

3. Individual students may lack the motivation to work alone.

4. Some students develop a poor estimation of self-esteem if they experience slow progress or failure.

5. The Laboratory strategy may cause the teacher to supervise individuals to the exclusion of the group.

6. Costs may exceed the benefits.

7. Unless well organized, it can become wasted time and effort on the part of all concerned.

8. Learning may become mechanical and passive.

9. This method is difficult to apply to all curricula.

10. It is difficult to develop projects so that all students have equally challenging activities and experiences.

11. The teacher may face problems because of the uneven starting and stopping points.

Guidelines for Maximum Utilization

1. The use of this strategy requires close planning and coordination between the teacher and the learner.

2. The approval of projects must be within the capability of the student, teacher and academic situation.

3. Know that Laboratory requires flexibility on your part and in the learning environment.

4. Care must be taken to see that appropriate materials and supplies are available.

5. The teacher must select appropriate criteria in advance for the final evaluation of the students' projects.

6. Arrange approval by the administration for questionable projects.

7. Relate the results to previously studied material.

8. Establish time limits for completion of Laboratory work.

9. Don't allow the project to become busy work.

10. Plan alternative activities for those who finish their Laboratory work earlier than anticipated.

11. Students should maintain a lab notebook or log of accomplishments.

Summary

If Laboratory experiences are not always limited to "cookbook experiments" (Place a drop of iodine on the bread. What color does the bread become? _____ What does this mean? _____), they can give students the opportunity to *do* learning as opposed to reading about other people's learning. Retention and interest will increase exponentially and opportunities for creative thought can be exercised.

Success is determined mostly by teacher preparation and direction appropriate to the learner's ability. *Some* structure is definitely necessary if predictable results are desired. It is important to remember that Laboratory learning teaches process as well as production.

Questions to Promote Discussion

1. What advantage to learning does the Laboratory approach offer that no other approach offers? Explain.

2. In your estimation, what is the most glaring inadequacy of the Laboratory strategy? Explain why.

3. Is there any way to compensate for the inadequacy noted in answer to Question #2? Why, or why not?

LEARNING PACKETS

Definition and Description

The Unipac, Lappak, Learn-a-pac, and others are sets of self-contained learning materials assembled for the purpose of teaching a single concept or idea. They are generally structured for individual use and are most effectively used in schools with flexible curricula, although they are not limited to these settings. The Learning Packet may be an excellent means of initiating *individualized learning*.

The unit package consists of a series of sequential learning activities leading to the achievement of desired outcomes (stated in behavioral terms) by the learners. Components of the Learning Packets may include:

-Teacher directions
-Student instructions
-Pre-test
-Major and sub-concepts
-Behavioral objectives
-Assorted strategies and content
-Student self-assessment
-Post-test
-Research activities
-Independent resource and study materials

The Learning Packet is designed to help students achieve at their own best learning rate. The teacher is a resource person available to offer assistance as the student pursues the learning content of the instructional package.

Because the unit is designed for individual use, a series of units may be developed on a single topic area. Each must be of increasing difficulty requiring the learner to develop new skills, techniques, and greater knowledge.

Advantages or Special Purposes

1. Students are able to pursue special interest areas yet still work within the confines of the total curriculum.

2. Learning takes place in a sequential order.

3. All concepts are stated in behavioral (measurable) terms.

4. Materials in Learning Packets can be developed for all levels of learning.

5. Any discipline can be the subject of Learning Packets.

6. Learning Packets may be exchanged both within the school and with other schools.

7. The Learning Packet is well planned from start to finish.

8. Using the pre-test and post-test, the teacher is able immediately to evaluate the amount of learning that has taken place.

9. Teachers are placed in the role of facilitators of learning rather than directors of learning.

10. Students gain broader insight into learning through the use of varied materials and activities and by doing research in their special interest areas.

Disadvantages or Limitations

1. Unit packets are time consuming to develop.

2. They are often misused as testing devices rather than learning units.

3. The Learning Packet requires an abundance of resource materials in order to complete the total project.

4. Teachers tend to treat unit packages as isolated projects rather than as part of the total curriculum.

5. Students may tend to get bored with lengthy learning units.

6. Students may not have the maturity to work independently.

Guidelines for Maximum Utilization

1. Take time to understand thoroughly how to develop and use Learning Packets.

2. Take the time to work through the unit prior to classroom use, to be sure it is complete and accurate.

3. Plan well in advance to see that all necessary materials and resources are available.

4. Follow the directions for teachers within the Learning Packet.

5. Establish a definite time period for completion of the unit of learning.

6. Confer with each student as he or she progresses, to clarify activities and to provide continuous assessment.

7. Relate the Learning Packet to the curriculum. (Do not allow it to become isolated from learning goals.)

8. Check to assure yourself that the school organization has the required flexibility to pursue this type of learning activity.

Summary

If a teacher ever desired to have learning materials pre-packaged, those prayers have been answered. The Learning Packet is complete from beginning to end except for the inclusion of a motivation pill for the student. This job is left up to the teacher, as always. "Facilitation" by the teacher means proper direction and explanation before the student begins the unit, encouragement and guidance during involvement, and proper supervision of evaluation and unit conclusion. Encouragement and positive reinforcement are important to the success of this strategy since only a minority of public school age students is totally self-motivating in independent work.

Above all, the teacher must have a thorough understanding of each Learning Packet. Since there are specific instructions for the teacher, they should be adhered to strictly.

Questions to Promote Discussion

1. Which do you feel to be the wiser course of action: buying commercially prepared Learning Packets or developing your own? Why?

2. If you were to consider using Learning Packets, what do you believe would be the major problem to face? Why?

3. What steps would you take to overcome the problem elicited in the preceding question?

4. What do you consider to be the unique feature of using Learning Packets? Why?

THE LECTURE

Definition and Description

The Lecture is the traditional method of teaching wherein the lecturer transmits information in an autocratic fashion to passive student listeners. In the pure form, students have no opportunity to ask questions or offer comments during the Lecture.

Advantages or Special Purposes

1. The Lecture is most helpful in introducing a new topic of study or presenting certain background material that students need for preparation or further study.

2. Lecture permits auditory learners to receive succinct information quickly about aspects of materials that will increase their understanding of what lies ahead.

3. Lecture provides students who are auditory learners with an organized perspective of the content to be considered.

4. Lecture provides practice for the students in learning to develop note-taking skills.

5. The Lecture provides the teacher with a sense of "security" since information to be covered is established in advance.

Disadvantages or Limitations

1. Lengthy or overly frequent lectures can easily lead to boredom.

2. The lecturer has difficulty in assessing impact on the audience and whether student needs and interests are being met.

3. Individuals in the group are not permitted to ask questions, thus eliminating feedback and leading to miscommunication.

4. Detailed and factual information is difficult to "communicate" or "relate" in such a setting.

5. Affective learning seldom occurs and kinesthetic learning never occurs as the result of a Lecture.

6. Higher level cognitive learning is seldom achieved by students since they do not actively work with the information being considered.

Guidelines for Maximum Utilization

1. Know the overall goals and specific objectives while planning the Lecture.

2. Know the audience. What are their specific needs and interests? Goals should then mesh with these needs and interests in order to eliminate boredom and to help students grow.

3. The Lecture should be well organized so that the logic is as "perceivable" as possible. This includes planning of methodology, utilization of equipment, demonstration materials, handouts, etc.

4. Vary the Lecture by using interest-arousing aids such as pictures, models and other visuals. The chalkboard serves as a useful tool for outlining or emphasizing important points.

5. Avoid monotonous-type lecturing by varying voice stress and intensity. Try to stir students' imaginations by painting with vivid word images.

6. Avoid "pure" Lecture by utilizing questions during the Lecture. Two kinds of questions may be used: (1) the kind you ask---pause---and answer yourself (rhetorical), and (2) the kind you expect students to answer. Both are attention-getters and the second has the added benefit of requiring mental answer-search on the part of the students as well as providing a feedback mechanism to enable the lecturer to measure audience absorption.

7. Always allow ample opportunity for questions to come from the students.

8. Watch the audience. Their actions (attentiveness) will reveal the effectiveness of the lecture.

9. After the Lecture, attempt to break into *cooperative learning groups* to develop clarification of the materials discussed. The lecturer should circulate from group to group.

10. Revise Lecture approach on the basis of feedback (6, 7, 8, and 9 above).

Summary

Lecture: the oldest form of teaching and one of the most ineffective---ineffective because it is overused, abused, and misused. Lectures should be short, sweet, and to the point - when they are necessary at all. Generally speaking, Lectures are ineffective because they place the learner in a very passive posture. This lack of activity is extremely conducive to boredom and daydreaming, and it sometimes spawns discipline problems. Lecture assumes that the lecturer knows all and the "lecturee" is ignorant, and this automatically turns off some listeners.

The degree to which this happens is determined to some extent by the attitude of the lecturer while making the presentation.

Lecture is most effective in clarifying or demonstrating a procedure or skill.

Questions to Promote Discussion

1. For years many educators and students have been extremely critical of the overuse of Lectures. However, the Lecture approach is still overused. Why?

2. What is the chief limitation of the Lecture? Why?

3. What should the teacher do to overcome this limitation?

OBSERVATION

Definition and Description

Observation is probably more of a teacher skill than a strategy. However, its importance is so crucial to effective use of other strategies and it is so intricately intertwined with all of them that it becomes almost imperative to treat it as a "pure form" strategy.

An "observer" is usually thought of as an unobtrusive person sitting in the corner passively watching students. It is a rare teacher who has the luxurious opportunity to observe his own students perform. Therefore, we shall define Observation as "astute perception by the teacher of multi-faceted student behavior, attitudes, and learning problems while in the midst of a dynamic classroom situation." In other words, the teacher should be aware of "what's happening." To be constantly cognizant of what is transpiring throughout the class is not an easy task. It is especially difficult for those teachers who are in the habit of seeing "the group" rather than the individuals who compose the group. It is of utmost importance to be "omnisciently observant," as this is the major and only *immediate* way to learn of student reactions to the general environment and particular learning segments.

Advantages or Special Purposes

1. Through Observation much can be learned concerning student physiological problems (hearing, vision, speech, coordination, bodily defects, etc.) and needs (diet supplements, hygiene care, clothing, etc.).

2. Observation yields a great deal of information about the learner's socio-emotional development.

3. The data supplied by the two above practices are necessary for the teacher's precise observance of student's academic problems. For example, if the student is observed to be having an academic difficulty, does the cause lie in the student's

physiological/socio-emotional realms or does it arise from teacher/subject matter areas (lack of student readiness, improper or unclear directions, irrelevant or uninteresting material or methods, etc.)?

4. Observation provides immediate information and feedback, whereas testing or diagnostics lessen the effect of problem-attention due to the time-delay.   Many potential learning problems can be eliminated by prompt action, ultimately saving a great deal of energy and discomfort on the part of both teacher and student.

5. Keen observations eliminate many discipline problems before they occur.

6. The obvious interest displayed by the teacher leaves no doubt in the students' minds that the instructor is concerned about them.   This provides for a mutually pleasant and positive learning environment and tends to increase growth in all domains.

7. As the teacher becomes increasingly aware of the effects of various strategies in different situations (and alters teaching approaches on the basis of that information) she becomes a true self-improving professional, constantly seeking a better way.

Disadvantages or Limitations

1. It is difficult to become a sharp observer.   It requires determined practice at separating oneself into two people---a person "teaching" (demonstrating, lecturing, utilizing AV material, passing out papers, etc.) and a person "observing"(alert to physiological, socio-emotional, learning and behavioral aspects).

2. It is difficult to be objective; we all tend to feel "I am objective, but they are not."   This usually false predisposition

prevents the teacher from examining his/her own observational objectivity.

3. There is a tendency to "play favorites," to observe only children who are pleasing to watch.

4. There is a tendency to watch for only negative occurrences, thereby failing to notice and accentuate positive traits being exhibited.

5. The inclination is to be solely on the alert for particulars, which can lead to failure to sense the total classroom atmosphere.

Guidelines for Maximum Utilization

1. The teacher should plan on the necessary self-training in Observation skills. A daily skill goal should be established and carried out in all contacts with students. Some sample goals might be:

Day 1: Which students appear to pay attention? When?
Day 2: Which students appear not to pay attention? When?
Day 3: What habits (repeated behaviors) are exhibited by which students?
Day 4: Which students appear to have vision difficulty? Hearing problems?
Day 5: Who are the isolates? How do they behave differently?
Day 6: Which students attempt to monopolize your attention? What methods do they use?
Day 7: What physical handicaps are present?
Day 8: Which students like to tease? How? To whom do they direct their teasing?
Day 9: Who dominates discussions? When?
Day 10: Who appears to need peer approval? How do they go about getting it? When?
Day 11: What rewards work best with which students?

Day 12:   What rewards work best with which students? (It takes
          at least two days.).
Day 13:   Which students cooperate with which other students?
          When?
Day 14:   Which students cooperate with you? When?
Day 15:   Who are the silent leaders? When?
Day 16:   Who appears to have difficulty with which subject matter
          (or particular part of the subject matter)?
Day 17:   Who asks questions? When? What kind?
Day 18:   Who appears to read with comprehension? When?
Day 19:   Who appears to be tired? When?
Day 20:   Who appears to get emotionally upset? When?

And the list could go on and on. Practice at looking for
particular traits or behaviors eventually sharpens the teacher's
observation powers beyond belief. The teacher's eye becomes
so discerning that a mountain of information can be compiled
with a few glances around the classroom.

2.   Observation should be as objective as possible. Until we have
     the ability to enter other people's minds to see actually why
     they do the things they do, we must restrict our descriptions to
     observable behavior.   This   eliminates   such   value-laden
     judgements as: "Bill was very *bad* when he..."; "Martha has an
     annoying habit of..."; and "Jane constantly has a *harmful effect*
     on..." Such prejudicial statements, although seemingly correct
     to the observer, may be extremely inaccurate, and can only lead
     to distortion of the true situation. Once this happens, corrective
     behavior by the teacher stands an excellent chance of being
     irrelevant,   and   probably   detrimental,   to   the   learning
     environment and the people involved.

3.   Only after one has carefully considered the evidence as to why
     certain student behavior is exhibited should one attempt to
     accentuate positive behavior and eliminate negative behavior
     through utilization of new learning strategies or positive
     disciplinary measures. (It is at this point that a program of
     behavior modification may be initiated.)

4. Never neglect your built-in "environmental thermostat.
    Despite looking for particular behaviors, you must constantl
    attune part of your observation powers to the classroor
    atmosphere. Is it conducive or detrimental to learning? Is i
    time to do something else - take a break, go on a field trip
    have free time, or change subject matter?

Summary

Observation is perception. Accurate perception is invaluable to th
proficient teacher. It might be the fundamental strategy underlyin,
effective use of all other strategies. How else is a teacher to judge whe:
and how to plug in different strategies if he/she is not gaining accurat
input on student needs and desires?

Most of us are fairly poor observers. Although the teacher i
supposed to reinforce students towards progress, who motivates th
teacher to improve? Usually not principals or paychecks. It is purely o:
the teacher's shoulders to be mature and professional enough to take
step and enjoy the feeling of "doing better." Observation, if practiced
can be one of the most rewarding steps ever taken, and it is the onl
means by which a teacher can become an expert "surfer of the chaos."

Questions to Promote Discussion

1. In your opinion, should "Observation" be included in a book o
    teaching strategies? Why or why not?

2. What is the major disadvantage or limitation of Observation
    Explain.

3. How would a teacher overcome the problem cited in answer t
    Question #2?

4. What can Observation, as described, most contribute to th
    teacher? Is that important? Explain.

5. How is Observation an integral aspect of Teacher Expectation and Student Achievement?

6. What Observation tools could be used in a *cooperative learning* model?

OUTCOME BASED EDUCATION (MASTERY LEARNING)

Definition and Description

Outcome Based Education or O.B.E. is used by many people to mean a variety of things. It is not new in education, but has come back into vogue recently. The basis for this new interest stems from D.J. Mueller's "mastery learning instructional model." The model includes the following basic components:

1. Formal development of a comprehensive set of cognitive objectives.

2. Instruction, using a variety of teaching methods.

3. Frequent assessment, both formal and diagnostic.

4. Corrective and/or remedial instruction.

5. Criterion-referenced summative evaluation (a review by testing over the entire process).

The objectives are first clearly specified for the lesson or unit to be learned. This is followed by the traditional instructional methods used in any classroom. After instruction, all students are tested for mastery of the specific objectives. Those students exhibiting deficiencies are given additional instruction and time to master the objectives of the lesson. The important aspect of O.B.E. is that a student must demonstrate competency before moving to the next learning segment.

Advantages or Special Purposes

1. The strategy can be used in any subject area.

2. Objectives are clearly listed prior to beginning the lesson.

3. The class works on the lesson as a group, with the teacher noting individual needs for special help at a later time.

4. The individual students do not feel singled out if they learn at a slower rate than their peers.

5. Specific needs of individuals are succinctly defined and treated without delay or lag time.

6. The strategy works equally well in corrective or remedial situations.

7. Mastery of initial and early units forms the basis for the next unit.

8. It tends to build confidence in the learner with each unit mastered.

9. Although the strategy is time consuming, the results are extremely satisfying when properly executed to a conclusion.

Disadvantages or Limitations

1. The programs used must be flexible enough to accommodate the wide disparity of abilities within the classroom.

2. Flexibility for meeting diverse cultural backgrounds is necessary and difficult to achieve in some subject areas.

3. Teachers often lack the necessary expertise to carry out O.B.E. programs.

4. The Curriculum (subject) objectives must be clearly specified--- often a difficult and time-consuming task.

5. The strategy can be time consuming if student ability and achievement ranges are extremely wide.

6. Evaluation and follow-up instruction for remediation and corrective measures require explicit planning.

7. Paper work, record keeping and follow-up activities call fo assistance from teacher aides or peer tutors.

Guidelines for Maximum Utilization

1. Develop clear, sequential cognitive objectives for the specifi lesson and unit before beginning instruction.

2. Give clear directions and, preferably, an example of procedur to students before beginning the lesson. Evaluative criteri should also be made quite clear in advance.

3. Prepare to enter the O.B.E. strategy by experimenting with simple lesson before attempting more complex ones.

4. Formative tests must be prepared in advance for use at the en of a lesson or unit.

Summary

Outcomes and objectives are critical elements in the instructiona cycle. In its simplest terms Outcome Based Education or master learning requires that we identify what we want students to learn in th lesson, week and year. Outcomes can be written for any level o Bloom's taxonomy from memory level to synthesis and evaluation. The can be written for the cognitive, kinesthetic, and the affective domain They can also be evaluated in any manner from the traditional fill in th blank test to authentic or portfolio assessment and class presentations.

We know that students do not learn at the same rates and O.B.E recognizes that reality and allows students to proceed at different rate The delivery of instruction becomes individualized as teachers move awa from the traditional approach of everyone on the same page of the ext to the dynamics of teaching to the developmental needs of the individual child. The best delivery systems for Outcome Based Education allow students to remediate, practice, master and review learning outcomes as they proceed.

Learning outcomes can be identified by students, parents, citizens, board members and teachers alike. What a child learns in the classroom is not limited to the objectives identified. Certainly a multitude of knowledge, attitudes and values will surface in a classroom exchange. Teaching to objectives does not require that teachers ignore teachable moments and serendipity learning. All teachers teach to objectives. Those who are conscious of what students need to learn in order to enhance their learning have a better chance of ensuring that students are also conscious of what is important to learn.

Questions to Promote Discussion

1. What are the pros and cons of O.B.E. academically? Psychologically?

2. How does O.B.E. promote "accountability?"

3. What would a comprehensive set of cognitive objectives look like in your teaching field?

4. What instructional strategies would you most favor using in conjunction with O.B.E.? Why?

PROBLEM-SOLVING

Definition and Description

The name "problem-solving" is assigned to learning approaches based upon the scientific method of inquiry. These approaches are built upon John Dewey's five steps of general Problem-Solving: (1) defining the problem, (2) formulating tentative hypotheses, (3) collecting, evaluating, organizing, and interpreting data, (4) reaching conclusions, and (5) testing those conclusions. For example, a social studies class might become concerned about what will happen in Cuba when Castro dies. The problem then becomes: What happens to the dictatorship when a dictator dies?

The class members discuss various alternatives and then finally state their hypothesis: When a dictator dies, the dictatorship ends. Next, they would collect, evaluate, organize and interpret data. They would study dictators throughout history and what happened to the dictatorship upon the death of each dictator. The data might either support or deny the hypothesis.

Next a conclusion would be reached regarding what generally has happened to the dictatorship when the dictator dies. The degree to which the hypothesis is supported or denied by the evidence determines the conclusion. The conclusion would then be applied to Castro and a prediction could be made. (Time would enable the prediction to be tested.)

Advantages or Special Purposes

1. Due to the student's active involvement comprehension and retention should be of longer duration.

2. Problem-Solving provides the student with a model to apply to problems that may be faced in the future.

3. Problem-Solving involves cognitive (including higher levels) and affective learning.

4. Problem-Solving develops responsibility in the learner.

5. Interest in learning and motivation are increased with the use of Problem-Solving.

6. Students utilize materials and resources other than a single textbook.

7. Students learn how to think independently in reaching conclusions.

8. Problem-Solving provides the opportunity for students to learn from failure without severe hardships.

9. The student learns to accept the opinions of others.

Disadvantages or Limitations

1. Materials and resources needed for Problem-Solving often are not available to the students.

2. Problem-Solving can be time consuming.

3. Students may tend to become negative in outlook, thinking that the only worthwhile area of study is a "problem."

4. Students are often too immature to really recognize problems of social significance.

5. The teacher must be very well prepared in the discipline.

6. The issues that are controversial in nature may create problems with administrators, parents or community groups.

7.   Evaluation of learning can be difficult.

Guidelines for Maximum Utilization

1.   Expose the student to a number of similar problems.

2.   The problems presented must fit the maturation and skill level of the student.

3.   The student must see the problem as being important.

4.   Assist pupils in defining and delimiting the problem to be studied.

5.   Check for sufficient resources and materials to be available for student use.

6.   Provide guidance and direction when necessary, taking care not to overdo it.

7.   Help students establish criteria with which to make appropriate evaluations.

Summary

Problem-Solving moves the mind to some of its highest cognitive functions: Analyzing, generalizing, and synthesizing. This alone justifies it as one of the most valuable of all strategies. Magnifying the value is accomplished if the problems to be solved are relevant and interesting to the students. It is impossible to overestimate the importance of topic selection and preparation/planning. The teacher would be wise to assess, by oral or written survey, the interests of pupils prior to topic selection. Ms. Rosemary Daniell, a poet-in-residence on Lookout Mountain, wanted to find out the elementary children's real interests before selecting poetry topics. She found that the children were fascinated with three things, mainly death, dreams, and God. All of these were, of course, not in the school curriculum or in her thought list. The shift to these topics was very rewarding. The children could not write enough poetry for Ms. Daniell, and motivation was no problem. The survey certainly was worth the little time and effort required.

An added benefit in utilizing this strategy is that students become adept at digging up information and cross-checking its validity with other resources. Critical thinking is a too infrequent exercise for most students and the Problem-Solving strategy is part of the solution of this dilemma.

Questions to Promote Discussion

1. Choose a problem and describe how the teacher could use the Problem-Solving approach in the classroom.

2. What do you consider to be the major advantage of the Problem-Solving approach? Why?

3. What do you consider to be the chief limitation of the Problem-Solving approach? Why?

4. How would you overcome the problem identified in response to Question #3?

PROGRAMMED LEARNING (INSTRUCTION)

Definition and Description

The *Dictionary of Education* describes Programmed Instruction as:

> instruction utilizing a workbook, textbook, or mechanical and/or electronic device programmed to help pupils attain a specific level of performance by (a) providing instruction in small steps, (b) asking one or more questions about each step in the instruction and providing instant knowledge of whether each answer is right or wrong, and (c) enabling pupils to progress at their own pace, either individually through self-pacing or as a team through group-pacing.

The psychological principles of Programmed Instruction are stimulus, response, and reinforcement. The small steps (frames) are designed in sequential arrangements and detail so that the student will generally make correct responses. These responses are then reinforced.

Auto-instruction and automated teaching are synonyms for Programmed Instruction. Machine teaching, often erroneously termed Programmed Instruction, is only one type of Programmed Instruction.

One method of programming is variously termed linear, fixed-sequence, straight-line, or extrinsic. In such an approach the units of content are designed in small sequential steps which must be completed in the pre-arranged order.

The other basic method of programming is called nonlinear, branching, or intrinsic. In this approach, the student responds to a presented step, or frame. The next frame the student faces depends upon his response. If correct, the student goes on to a new exercise. If incorrect, the student may be referred to remedial exercises.

Advantages or Special Purposes

1. Programmed Instruction saves the teacher a considerable amount of time.

2. The time saved can be applied to individuals or groups for either remedial or higher intellectual learning.

3. Programmed Instruction is effective for remedial teaching, drill and practice, as well as enrichment.

4. The learner is actively responding at all times to the program.

5. The student progresses at his/her own rate and level of achievement.

6. The success and reinforcement given the student provides motivation for the learner.

7. Research has demonstrated that students can learn effectively through Programmed Instruction.

8. Students can study programs on their own which are not part of the ordinary curriculum.

9. The student, through immediate feedback, is aware of the degree of progress being made.

Disadvantages or Limitations

1. Good programs are hard to identify and not all programs on the market are worth using.

2. Writing programs is a very difficult process which generally causes teachers to rely on commercial programs.

3.   The kinds of materials and types of learning which can be programmed are limited.   For example, the material must be that which contains a right answer.

4.   Programmed Instruction is not very applicable to affective or kinesthetic learning.

5.   The cost of materials and/or machines can be prohibitive.

6.   Some students complain that programs are dull, boring or repetitious.

7.   Programmed Instruction for individual development does not fit the school's structure of time, semesters, credit hours, etc.

Guidelines for Maximum Utilization

1.   Thoroughly study the objectives of the program to be sure they fit the objectives of the teacher.

2.   Completely work through the program in order to check out its applicability and to better understand what the student will experience.

3.   Use programmed materials to meet the individual needs of students.

4.   Begin utilizing programs for a unit of content, then evaluate the experience to decide upon further use.

5.   Programmed Instruction is usually most effective when used periodically rather than all of the time.

6.   Students can learn much by actually making their own programs. A side benefit of this is that excellently constructed programs can be used with future students.

Summary

For a time Programmed Learning was the rage. Total courses were taught with this strategy. The rage subsided and so did the utilization of Programmed Instruction. In a way, it's not surprising---this is the usual pattern in education; a new fad is overused to the point of negating its value. This is unfortunate. A course with Programmed Instruction as the sole method of learning can be devastatingly boring and tedious, but properly used on a once-in-a-while basis it can be fun and provides variety. It is especially useful in science and mathematics, and materials can be found or constructed for all learner levels, whether slow, average, or gifted.

Materials can be bought, teacher-made, student-made, or borrowed. They can be reused (if separate answer sheets are dittoed) year after year, and rarely need updating as they usually cover basic concepts (magnetism, Civil War, long division, etc.).

The biggest point in favor of Programmed Instruction is that it is another method in the arsenal of *individualized learning*, an overall strategy heartily endorsed by the authors.

Questions to Promote Discussion

1. There was a time when some people believed the computer (utilizing programs) would replace the classroom teacher. This did not happen. What disadvantages or limitations of Programmed Instruction do you feel contributed to this? Why?

2. In what ways can Programmed Instruction be a real benefit to the student? To the teacher?

3. Name a specific subject area. Now list the ways in which you could apply Programmed Instruction.

PROJECT

Definition and Description

The *Dictionary of Education* describes the project method as "a teaching in which students individually or in groups accept an assignment to gather and integrate data relative to some problem and are then free to fulfill the requirements independently of the teacher, who furnishes help only when necessary." The Project approach may be referred to as self-directed study.

This method requires teaching by units rather than by pages. The decision as to the nature of the project can be assigned by the teacher, or it can evolve from class discussions.

Advantages or Special Purposes

1. The Project approach covers all levels of the cognitive and affective domains.

2. Pupils can be involved in planning the Project, thus increasing interest and motivation.

3. Emphasis is placed upon *doing* by the student.

4. The Project method develops student responsibility and initiative.

5. The student develops greater understanding of *how* to learn.

6. This strategy permits a study of broader areas because of the individual efforts or desires of the class.

Disadvantages or Limitations

1. Projects are very time consuming.

2. Projects are often little more than busy work and, therefore, students may seem to be learning much more than is the case.

3. Students, due to academic immaturity, often make many errors.

4. Often the materials and resources needed to facilitate an effective Project are limited.

5. Students often get sidetracked or go off on a tangent.

6. Helpful teacher feedback usually is not possible until it is too late, i.e., at grade time.

Guidelines for Maximum Utilization

1. Be certain that sufficient resources and/or materials are available before undertaking Projects.

2. Great care must be taken in the selection of the Project. Students should be helped in finding Projects which have meaning for them but which are also meaningful in terms of the goals of the subject.

3. Be sure the Project is specifically defined and understood by the students involved. Establish objectives for each Project at the outset.

4. Provide enough supervision to ensure maximum progress, but not so much as to rob students of meaningful learning experiences.

5. Let the students evaluate their Project prior to any teacher evaluation.

6. Provide an opportunity to utilize *community resources*.

7. Evaluate according to agreed upon objectives.

Summary

Projects are usually done by individuals and frequently take the form of a model or presentation as the final product. If a Project involves in-depth work, it becomes research (see *student research).* Well known examples of Projects are seen at science fairs. In geography, students may make globes, or papier-mache relief maps. In mathematics, puzzles, models, or games may be created. Sometimes projects are creative but often they are duplicative of something previously done.

Projects give students the opportunity to work independently and to gain in-depth knowledge of a specific area.

Group Projects sometimes take the form of a large-scale city map, play production, jury trial, large model construction, model grocery store, etc. The advantages of group Projects are that students must agree on division of labor, learn to lead or follow, and give and take criticism among themselves, as well as learn together about specific subject matter.

Questions to Promote Discussion

1. As a student, what are/were your personal reactions to "doing a Project?" Explain.

2. What do you consider to be the major advantage of the Project method? Why?

3. What do you consider to be the chief problem associated with the Project method? Why?

4. What steps could you take to overcome or minimize the chief problem of the Project method?

QUESTIONING

Definition and Description

Questioning, sometimes referred to as the question-and-answer method, is defined as "a method both of instruction and of oral testing based on teacher-formulated questions to be answered by the students."

Advantages or Special Purposes

1. In using questions the teacher must be aware of the purposes to which they may be correctly applied. Callahan lists the following classifications of the purposes of questions (Sterling G. Callahan, *Successful Teaching in Secondary Schools*):
   a. Stimulate analytical thought.
   b. Diagnose student difficulties.
   c. Determine progress toward specific goals.
   d. Motivate students.
   e. Clarify and expand concepts.
   f. Encourage new appreciations and attitudes.
   g. Give specific direction to thinking.
   h. Relate cause to effect.
   i. Encourage student self-evaluation.
   j. Encourage the application of concepts.

2. Aschner, in his book, *Strategies and Tactics in Secondary School Teaching: A Book of Readings*, believes that teachers use questions to stimulate four types of thinking activities. The types are: remembering, reasoning, evaluating or judging, and creative thinking.

3. In a similar manner, questions may be designed in terms of Bloom's *Taxonomy of Educational Objectives: Cognitive Domain*. Such questions may be organized to serve the purpose of measuring learning on the levels of information, comprehension, application, analysis, synthesis or evaluation.

4. In the instructional process, questions can serve as a means of feedback for the teacher. This feedback can be either in terms of the understanding of an individual student or the understanding of the total class.

5. Lastly, questions are sometimes used as a control device in the sense that when students know that they may be called upon at any time, they are more apt to pay attention to what is going on in class.

Disadvantages or Limitations

1. It is difficult to design questions to measure certain types of learning. It is easier to design questions which measure factual learning than those which measure analysis, synthesis, and evaluation.

2. It is the ease of designing factual questions which leads teachers often to ignore planning questions in advance; thus most questions asked by teachers tend to be factual in nature. Students feel encouraged to memorize, neglecting higher learning levels.

3. Several incorrectly answered questions often prompt teachers to feel more time should be spent lecturing than questioning. This is partially caused by the threat to the teacher's ego. Who wants to feel he or she has not been successful in teaching?

4. Consistently answering questions incorrectly may lead to a lowered self-concept for the student.

5. Teachers tend to question high achievers more often than low achievers (see *TESA*).

Guidelines for Maximum Utilization

Whatever the purpose of the questions to be asked by the teacher, the responsibility of the teacher is first to plan properly and then to execute effectively. In planning, the teacher should:

1. Decide upon the purposes of the questions to be used.

2. Structure, in advance, the more difficult types of questions to be used. It is desirable to take the time to write out such questions on note cards or the margins of the text.

3. If questions are to be used for either review or preassessment purposes, be sure to sample class responses randomly.

4. Use "who," "what," "when," and "where" questions to check information possessed by students. For higher thought levels, use "why" and "how" questions.

5. Push students' responses to "why and "how" questions to higher levels of thought by asking for more explanation.

6. When using questions with individuals, state the question, pause, then call on a student to answer. This leads all students to listen to the question. The pause provides time to think---respect that period of silence.

7. Summarize complicated or ambiguous answers to questions.

8. Ask questions of all students equally.

9. If a student repeatedly provides incorrect answers coach that child to success "one-on-one" and tell them "tomorrow I will ask you this question."

10. Be equitable and reasonable in the use of "good," or other words of praise to students who give correct answers. Do not

belittle incorrect answers---this is the surest way to create low response on future questioning.

11. Allow students the opportunity to formulate questions in response to answers from the teacher or other students.

12. Questions can be used in connection with games such as "Bees" or the class's own version of "Jeopardy."

13. Use higher level questions with all students equitably, coach students to succeed.

Summary

An effective question-asker is as beautiful to watch (listen to) as a fencer. He/she knows when and what to ask. His/her questions demand thinking, not just factual recall. It takes a certain measure of ego-elimination on the part of the teacher to relinquish the desire to furnish all the answers.

Good Questioning techniques aid and stimulate the listener to reason, evaluate, and even create. Inspiration is given by the teacher for the student to move beyond memorizing thought functions to higher levels of thinking. Very important, obviously, is positive reinforcement of answers symbolizing "good thinking" if one wishes it to continue.

Questions to Promote Discussion

1. Imagine a teacher instructing a class session using only Questions. What would be some outcomes of that session for the students? Explain.

2. What is the major difficulty teachers have in using Questions? How could you overcome these difficulties?

ROLE-PLAYING

Definition and Description

The *Dictionary of Education* explains Role-playing as "an instructional technique involving a spontaneous portrayal (acting out) of a situation, condition, or circumstances by selected members of a learning group." The situation to which the person responds may be either structured or unstructured.

A mock job interview in which the student is aware of the questions ahead of time exemplifies a structured situation. Using unusual or surprise questions in the interview would be unstructured for the student and would require spontaneity.

Advantages or Special Purposes

1. In Role-playing the student expresses feeling and attitudes.

2. Role-playing encourages creativity.

3. This method provides the student with the opportunity to "feel" the situation rather than merely intellectualize about it.

4. The student is motivated.

5. Students are being prepared for actual situations to be faced.

6. How students fit into their roles gives an indication of their knowledge of the situation.

7. Role-playing can be used to develop social skills.

8. Affective learning can be taught and/or effectively evaluated.

9. A system of communication based on action rather than words is used.

10. Role-playing provides an opportunity to pretest ideas of significance for future reference.

11. One learns to organize thoughts and responses instantly while reacting to a situation or question.

12. Students learn to remain calm in the face of adversity or pressure.

Disadvantages or Limitations

1. Students sometimes emphasize performance over the intended lesson.

2. Role-playing is time consuming.

3. Some students are unable to identify with the characters or situation.

4. Those students with talent often monopolize the situation.

5. Students often get "carried away" in their roles, which can lead to disruption of the class or distortion of the learning.

6. "Hot topics" and controversial issues often get out of hand in Role-playing.

7. This method may be harmful to those students who lack the necessary skills (those who are shy, or those who have speech problems).

8. Role-playing sometimes turns out to be a "dud" if it fails to relate to the student or lesson intended.

9. Playing roles demands some imagination on the part of the individual students involved.

10. Role-playing may benefit only the actual participants unless the objectives for the class have been clearly specified.

Guidelines for Maximum Utilization

1. Design the situation being utilized in sufficient detail in advance of the class session.

2. Define the *roles* in terms of the situation, keeping in mind student characteristics. (Actually, doing both numbers 1 and 2 in written form will be worth the effort.)

3. The actors should be given a short time to get their thoughts together.

4. The class members who are to observe should take notes and be instructed in what to look for.

5. Upon completion of the activity, evaluation of the students' performance should take place.

6. Certain portions of the activity may be improved with re-enactment.

7. In a "hot" display in which emotions get out of hand, a simple reversal of roles can accomplish much.

8. An atmosphere of freedom and security must exist in the classroom.

9. Here are ideas that you may want to choose in using the Role-playing strategy. The creative teacher will also think of many others that meet the needs in a specific situation.

Business
1. A labor representative negotiates a sensitive issue with the plant manager.

2.   An employee asks his/her boss for a raise.

Education
1.   A teacher encounters an irate parent
2.   A hostile student threatens a teacher.

Humanities
1.   An atheist encounters an evangelist.
2.   A contemporary poet argues poetic theory with a Victorian poet.

Science
1.   A fundamentalist Christian encounters a biologist who is teaching evolution.
2.   An environmentalist debates an energy expert.

Social Service
1.   Two children tell their eighty-year-old mother that she is being put in a home for the aged.
2.   A white policeman harasses an Hispanic in the barrio (good for a role reversal).

Role-play situations especially for children:
1.   The owner of a factory that is polluting the stream encounters a fisherman; a stockholder in the factory; the mayor of the town where the factory is located; and a fish.
2.   A teacher meets with an overactive student who cannot sit still.
3.   A man with two noisy dogs in his backyard meets with a neighbor who doesn't like the noise.
4.   George Washington meets with a soldier who wants to go home from the camp at Valley Forge.

To involve the entire class when a Role-play strategy is used, the following questions are suggested as a means of providing a class evaluation of the situation.

1.   How realistic was the performance of each character?

2. In what ways could the roles have been played differently?
3. How has the presentation changed your thinking about the characters portrayed?
4. What was the objective of the lesson portrayed?

Summary

Role-play has a unique value in that it is the only strategy that gets the student into another "identity," thus allowing him/her an opportunity to perceive how others might feel, think and act.   This is especially useful in helping students understand the circumstances of different ethnic and cultural backgrounds.

Another valid use for Role-playing is in a problem-solving situation where different roles are placed in conflict with each other.   This is utilized well in teacher education preparation classes where scenes such as problem child-parent-teacher, or principal-teacher-angry parent can be experienced.

It is highly recommended that the role-players thoroughly understand their roles, the limits of the roles and the situation of the scene prior to enactment.   This eliminates straying or turning a learning situation into a comedy.

Questions to Promote Discussion

1. Role-playing is often viewed as "fun" by students. How can you ensure that the "fun" is a real learning experience?

2. What is the major difficulty in using Role-playing in the class? Why?

3. What could you do to overcome this difficulty?

4. What do you consider to be the major use of Role-playing in the classroom? Why?

SIMULATION GAMING

Definition and Description

Simulation is an elaborate type of role-playing, gaming, and socio drama in which students simulate models of real-life situations. It invite. participants to develop decision-making competencies while striving fo established objectives, usually using competition between two teams o achieving a score which can be compared to an established norm score

Simulation games are produced by commercial enterprises but ca be designed by the classroom teacher. Generally the teacher devises rule and objectives for the game and provides roles for various students.

Advantages or Special Purposes

1. Simulation is appealing, motivates intense effort, and increase. learning.

2. Success or failure is rapidly and readily recognizable.

3. Vividness, meaning, and potential for greater retention an added.

4. Simulation has demonstrated its power to generate dee emotional involvement.

5. Learning to act by acting, learning to make decisions b making decisions, and learning to solve problems by solvin problems are developed.

6. Simulation is particularly effective with under-motivate children.

7. Simulation allows for manipulation by simplifying th complexity of what the game represents thus providing fo control of extraneous factors that exist in the real situation.

8. Simulation can be used for the acquisition of information, improvement of new processes, and identification of alternatives in decision-making.

9. Games lengthen the attention span and develop persistent application to work.

10. Optional starting and stopping times are distinct advantages.

11. Pupils learn to cope with unpredictable circumstances.

12. Games illustrate vividly the relationship between decision-making and its consequences.

13. The need for constant communication between players encourages social integration/interaction.

14. Games are effective in teaching values and attitudes.

15. Simulation provides for critiques of solutions, successes, mistakes, and decisions made.

16. The cost and time necessary for integration/carryover into the real world are reduced.

Disadvantages or Limitations

1. At best, simulation is very artificial and oversimplified.

2. Games can place too much emphasis on competition.

3. Models are too rigid and this can lessen their applicability.

4. Simulation takes too long to get to the heart of a lesson.

5. Teachers employing Simulation may be looked upon as allowing too much freedom and "disorder" in their classrooms.

6. Games cannot be readily adapted to the peculiar needs of ar individual or a particular class.

7. Gaming and role-playing often become activities for activity's sake and fail to provide for transfer; Simulation cannot be a substitute for real, direct experience.

8. Students who have minor roles may lose interest.

9. A complex model confuses; if it is overly simple, it bores.

10. The features represented and the outcomes to be achieved are predetermined by the designer who builds in his/her own biases

11. Time factors involved in Simulation Gaming do not always coincide with those time constraints under which the teache functions.

Guidelines for Maximum Utilization

If a commercially created Simulation game is utilized, then you need to be completely familiar with the game and prepare your class by: a) allowing sufficient time for the play; and b) carefully explaining the rule of the game.   All Simulation games include directions for play summarizing the activity, and relating it to "reality."

If you desire to construct your own Simulation situation, the following suggestions from Von Haden and King should be considered

1. In order to produce transferrable results, the model must posses fidelity in its representation of reality.

2. Purpose and major focus must be clearly understood.

3. Rules for Simulation games must be established.

4. The sophistication of the game usually increases its instructional potential.

5. Game designs must result from rigorous experimentation.

6. Simulation of all types should be evaluated in terms of the established objectives.

7. Learners in games must be free to carry out their own decisions, even when making mistakes, and the feedback of the consequences should be rapid and clear.

8. Opportunity and space must be provided for free, uninhibited movement and for flexibility of grouping.

9. An open climate should be maintained, free from leader domination.

10. The scope of the Simulation should be limited to selected critical aspects of actions or processes.

11. Creativity on the part of leaders and students is required.

12. Accurate information and facts are essential.

13. Reasonable assurance for intelligent use can be increased by setting significant goals and by previous testing.

14. Simulation should provide for teaching both the cognitive and the affective areas.

15. In the main, decisions must be sufficiently satisfying to provide adequate motivation.

16. Provision must be made for developing generalizations and/or summarizations.

17. The situation should be repeatable in its original form so tha
follow-up can be provided.

Summary

The greatest thing going for the Simulation Gaming strategy is it
intrinsic motivation. All kids love games, competition, and "winning.
Whether you feel this aspect is the major emphasis of Simulation or not
the children do.   Failure to capitalize on this enthusiastically wil
undermine all the preparation and time you invested to get across the
"lesson."

The most frequent problem is getting started, and the second mos
frequent is rule interpretation as the game progresses. The teacher i
crucial to both of these; he/she must act as explainer of the game'
objectives and methods prior to play and as a referee during the game
A great deal of the success of the experience rests upon how well this i
done.

Sample Team-building Simulation

Whitewater---Student group is whitewater rafting and during a sudde
storm, the raft overturns in the river and much of the equipment is lost
It is getting dark and much colder. Survival is the issue. Students mus
select a survival strategy and rank order the items they must salvage fo
survival. Comes with a Facilitator's Guide providing all the instruction
necessary for the teacher to provide background information, facilitation
and processing afterwards. (Available from Aviat, 555 Briarwood Circle
Ann Arbor, MI 48108)

Sample Computer Simulations

To introduce you to computerized Simulation Games (which do not need
a lot of teacher supervision) two types are mentioned here. Details may
be purchased from the publishers or local software dealers.

SimCity Series
published by Maxis

SimCity---A computer simulation of a city planning adventure. Students fight crime and unemployment, control budgets, transit and population. Students create industry, shopping centers, parks, airports and more---either from scratch or by using the models provided. Comes with the SimCity Planning Commission Handbook.

SimEarth---Students take charge of an entire planet and guide life from its inception as single-celled microbes to a human civilization. Graphs and information windows reveal every detail of the planet's health.

SimLife---Students design plants and animals at the genetic level to influence how they appear, act, and eventually evolve. Students can play with food webs, mutations, extinctions, and genetic engineering.

Carmen Sandiego Series
published by Broderbund

Where in The World is Carmen Sandiego?---Students learn geography as they join the Acme Detective Agency to pursue the infamous Carmen Sandiego and her gang. Fast-paced action, flip humor, and amusing animations keep interest high. Includes on-screen World Almanac and Book of Facts to help decipher clues.

Where in Space is Carmen Sandiego?---Students become part of the Acme Detective Agency Intergalactic Division to catch elusive Carmen and her gang on a cosmic crime binge, stealing everything from sunspots to Saturn's rings. Utilizes dazzling NASA photos, digitized sounds and music, 32 locations and over 1100 clues.

Where in the USA is Carmen Sandiego?---Students are part of the Acme Detective Agency in pursuit of notorious Carmen and her gang of 15 villains as they try to swipe America's most precious treasures and landmarks. Along the way students gain a totally enjoyable geography lesson with 50 topographic state maps, over 50 digitized location photos, and six talking characters.

Where in History is Carmen Sandiego?---History lessons for student
in an appealing format as can be surmised from the other Carmen game

Questions to Promote Discussion

1. What is the major advantage or benefit to be found in
    Simulation Gaming? Why?

2. What is the chief limitation of this approach? Why?

3. Does the benefit listed in Question #1 outweigh the limitation
    named in Question #2? Why or why not?

4. Should Simulation Gaming be used more often in the
    classroom? Explain.

SOCRATIC

The *Dictionary of Education* describes the Socratic method as "a process of discussion led by the teacher to induce the learner to question the validity of his reasoning or to reach a sound conclusion." The strategy derives its name from the approach used by Socrates as he assumed the role of intellectual midwife.

The Socratic approach was built upon the assumption that knowledge was within the student and proper questioning and commentary could cause this knowledge to surface. Socrates, as teacher, attempted to follow the student's argument wherever it led.

The key to the Socratic approach is that the teacher's comments and questions must enable the students to discover meaning for themselves.

In a typical classroom situation, the teacher would use the Socratic approach when the situation arose. It would be necessary for a student to make a statement, often of a value nature which could be further pursued. The teacher would then enter into a dialogue with the student, following the argument until the student had thoroughly questioned the answer and gained some insight into the logic used or the attitudes and beliefs held.

An example seems almost imperative to further explain the Socratic strategy. The following dialogue finds Socrates awaiting his own trial for impiety. He is seeking knowledge concerning piety from Euthyphro, who is supposedly knowledgeable of such matters.

Socrates: I know that, dear friend; and that is the reason why I desire to be your disciple. For I observe that no one, not even Meletus appears to notice you; but his sharp eyes have found me out at once, and he has indicted me for impiety. And, therefore, I adjure you to tell me the nature of piety and impiety, which you said that you knew so well, and of murder and the rest of them. What are they? Is not piety in every action always the same? and

impiety, again, is not that always the opposite of piety, and also the
same with itself, having, as impiety, one notion which includes
whatever is impious?

Euthyphro: To be sure, Socrates.

Socrates: And what is piety, and what is impiety?

Euthyphro: Piety is doing what I am doing; that is to say
prosecuting any one who is guilty of murder, sacrilege, or of any
other similar crime---whether he be your father or mother, or some
other person, that makes no difference---and not prosecuting them i
impiety. And please to consider, Socrates, what a notable proof
will give you of the truth of what I am saying, which I have already
given to others:---of the truth, I mean, of the principles that the
impious, whoever he may be, ought not to go unpunished. For de
not men regard Zeus as the best and most righteous of the gods?--
even they admit, that he bound his father (Cronos) because he
wickedly devoured his sons, and that he too had punished his own
father (Uranus) for a similar reason, on a nameless manner. And ye
when I proceed against my father,they are angry with me. This i
their inconsistent way of talking when the gods are concerned, and
when I am concerned.

Socrates: May not this be the reason, Euthyphro, why I am charged
with impiety---that I cannot always [agree] with these stories abou
the gods? and therefore I supposed that people think me wrong
But as you who are well informed about them approve of them,
cannot do better than assent to your superior wisdom. For what else
can I say, confession as I do, that I know nothing of them. I wish
you would tell me whether you really believe that they are true?

Euthyphro: Yes, Socrates; and things more wonderful still, of which
the world is in ignorance.

Socrates: And do you really believe that the gods fought with one
another, and had dire quarrels, battles, and the like, as the poets say
and as you may see represented in the works of great artists?

The temples are full of them; and notably the robe of Athene, which is carried up to the Acropolis at the great Panathenaea, is embroidered with them.   Are all these tales of the gods true, Euthyphro?

Euthyphro: Yes, Socrates, and, as I was saying, I can tell you, if you would like to hear them, many other things about the gods which would quite amaze you.

Socrates: I dare say; and you shall tell me them at some other time when I have leisure. But just at present I would rather hear from you a more precise answer, which you have not as yet given, my friend, to the question, What is "piety?" In reply, you only say that piety is, doing as you do, charging your father with murder?

Euthyphro: And that is true, Socrates.

Socrates: I dare say, Euthyphro, but there are many other pious acts.

Euthyphro: There are.

Socrates: Remember that I did not ask you to give me two or three examples of piety, but to explain the general idea which makes all pious things to be pious. Do you not recollect that there was one idea which made the impious impious and the pious pious?

Euthyphro: I remember.

Socrates: Tell me what this is, and then I shall have a standard to which I may look, and by which I may measure the nature of actions, whether yours or anyone's else, and say that this action is pious, and that impious?

Euthyphro: I will tell you if you like.

Socrates: I should very much like that.

Euthyphro: Piety, then is that which is dear to the gods and impiet is that which is not dear to them.

Socrates: Very good, Euthyphro; you have now given me just th sort of answer which I wanted. But whether it is true or not cannot as yet tell, although I make no doubt that you will prove th truth of your words.

Euthyphro: Of course.

Socrates: Come, then, and let us examine what we are saying. Tha thing, or person which is dear to the gods is pious, and that thing o person which is hateful to the gods is impious. Was not that said

Euthyphro: Yes that was said.

Socrates: And that seems to have been very well said too?

Euthyphro: Yes, Socrates, I think that; it was certainly said.

Socrates: And further, Euthyphro, the gods were admitted to hav enmities and hatreds and differences---that was also said?

Euthyphro: Yes, that was said.

Socrates: And what sort of difference creates enmity and anger Suppose for example that you and I, my good friend, differ about number; do differences of this sort make us enemies and set us a variance with one another? Do we not go at once to calculation, an end them by a sum?

Euthyphro: True.

Socrates: Or suppose that we differ about magnitudes, do we n quickly put an end to that difference by measuring?

Euthyphro: That is true.

Socrates: And we end a controversy about heavy and light by resorting to a weighing-machine?

Euthyphro: To be sure.

Socrates: But what differences are those which, because they cannot be thus decided, make us angry and set us at enmity with one another? I dare say the answer does not occur to you at the moment, and therefore I will suggest that this happens when the matters of difference are the just and unjust, good and evil, honorable and dishonorable: There would have been no quarrels among them, if there had been no such differences---would there now?

Euthyphro: You are quite right.

Socrates: Does not every man love that which he deems noble and just and good, and hate the opposite of them?

Euthyphro: Very true.

Socrates: But then, as you say, people regard the same thing, some as just and others as unjust; and they dispute about this, and there arise wars and fighting among them.

Euthyphro: Yes, that is true.

Socrates: Then the same things, as appears, are hated by the gods and loved by the gods, and are both hateful and dear the them?

Euthyphro: True.

Socrates: Then upon this view the same things, Euthyphro, will be pious and also impious?

Euthyphro: That, I suppose, is true.

Socrates: Then, my friend, I remark with surprise that you have nc
answered what I asked. For I certainly did not ask what was tha
which is at once pious and impious; and that which is loved by th
gods and also to be hated by them. And therefore, Euthyphro, i
thus chastising your father you may very likely be doing what i
agreeable to Zeus but disagreeable to Cronos or Uranus, and wha
is acceptable to Hephaestus but unacceptable to Hera, and there ma
be other gods who have similar differences of opinion.

Advantages or Special Purposes

1. The Socratic approach can be used in dealing with higher leve
    cognitive and affective learning.

2. The Socratic method gets the student to think about what is sai
    so that he/she can really examine an issue in depth.

3. The degree of teacher involvement can motivate the student.

4. Students are challenged when this technique is used properly

5. The strategy is transferable in that students can pursue thi
    technique in discussions with other students.

6. There is probably no strategy more suitable for promotin
    critical thinking than the Socratic.

Disadvantages or Limitations

1. It is difficult to formulate the kind of questions used in th
    Socratic approach.

2. The spontaneous nature of the Socratic approach can b
    threatening to the traditional role of the teacher.

3. This same spontaneity makes it difficult to be prepared.

4. Students often feel threatened when a teacher challenges their ideas.

5. While the teacher is in dialogue with one student, the other students in the class may lose interest.

6. It is difficult to assess a student's learning.

uidelines for Maximum Utilization

1. Prepare for the utilization of the Socratic approach by reading the *Republic*, the *Meno,* or some other work showing the teaching style of Socrates.

2. Begin by using the Socratic approach on a limited basis, preferably on attitudinal statements of students.

3. Assure students that you are attempting only to get them to re-think their ideas and that you are not criticizing them.

4. Be ready to shift gears if the attempt to use the Socratic approach bogs down.

5. Continue to develop skill in using the approach; this can only be done by attempting to use it.

6. When evaluating learning, give students the opportunity to show the logic of their viewpoints, and give credit accordingly.

7. Start with simple logic and gradually build to the complex.

ummary

The Socratic strategy enables the teacher to aid the student in xamining his/her own beliefs, values, attitudes and his or her logic or nconsistency. It is a difficult strategy to master and requires a friendly "let's-look-at-this" relationship. If this atmosphere is not present, th teacher's questioning will be viewed as picky and critical by the student thus negating the purpose of the strategy. Students need to comprehen the difference between criticizing and critical thinking for this strategy i work well.

Questions to Promote Discussion

1. What subject areas appear to you to be most compatible wi the Socratic approach? Why?

2. Select a subject area *not* listed in answer to Question #1. Ho could the Socratic method be used with this subject.

3. What is the key guideline to the proper use of the Socrat approach? Why?

STUDENT RESEARCH

Definition and Description

The research approach to teaching is defined in the *Dictionary of Education* as "an instructional procedure, the desired outcomes of which are achieved by setting up situations in such a form the student gathers and organizes information, draws his or her own conclusions on the basis of data, and compares his results with those obtained by other investigators."

The student may conduct this research in a laboratory situation or a non-laboratory situation or a combination of both. The non-laboratory research is usually library research, as in the social studies, performing surveys, etc.

The classroom focus of Student Research can be either upon the knowledge gained, the research skills and processes involved, or both.

Advantages or Special Purposes

1. Research conducted by the student leads the student to learn how a discipline is organized.

2. Student Research promotes student understanding of researcher methodologies in a particular field.

3. Research by students prepares them to direct their own learning in the future when faced with a new problem, e.g., developing an organizational structure for solution-seeking.

4. Research personalizes education in the sense that the student can research an area of interest or concern.

5.   Research can provide motivation as the student actively seeks answers.

6.   By using Research, the students must make judgments, reach conclusions, and report the findings.

7.   By conducting Research, the student not only learns content, but also develops various research skills.

8.   The student develops a sense of responsibility through conducting research.

Disadvantages or Limitations

1.   Research can be very time consuming.

2.   Research may require more materials and equipment than are available.

3.   Students, although initially motivated, may lose interest if the Research leads up blind alleys (topic too difficult, boring, or too lengthy).

4.   Immaturity or limited subject matter comprehension may cause students to have difficulty judging the importance of data acquired through Research.

5.   Students can easily become sidetracked or tangential in conducting Research.

6.   Students seldom get to work with primary sources or do original Research, thus giving them a distorted picture of what "real" Research involves.

Guidelines for Maximum Utilization

1. Decide beforehand whether the purpose of the research is the knowledge learned or the research process or both, and so inform the students.

2. Be sure the necessary materials, facilities and equipment for Research are available.

3. Base the type of Research upon the students' level of research sophistication.

4. Insist on students keeping extensive notes as the Research progresses.

5. Make certain the topics to be researched are well-defined and understood by the student.

6. Emphasize checks or student progress reports to ensure the direction of the Research.

7. Spend time helping students develop research skills before embarking upon a Research project.

8. Use as many primary sources as possible. Such research methods as *case studies*, *interview*, or sampling can help.

9. Provide students with opportunities to share their findings with peers.

10. Decide upon evaluation procedures in advance, and inform students of the criteria by which their efforts will be measured.

Summary

Research is highly interesting to some students and a total bore for others. Certain students thrive on the independence, the logicality and

definitiveness of this type of individual study while others may not. A
teacher must spend adequate preparatory time with the student in the
foundations of Research: (1) defining the "problem"; (2) gathering and
compiling data; (3) posing tentative solutions; and (4) developing note
taking and recording skills, etc.

A student doing Research needs input and the flexibility to make
contacts necessary for such input. This might be library time or first
hand gathering of information from local and state agencies.

The rewards of properly supervised and earnest carrying out of
Student Research can be great---thought organization, involvement
increased motivation, activism, in-depth knowledge of a specific area, and
feeling of accomplishment.

Questions to Promote Discussion

1.   What do you consider the major benefit of the Student Research
     approach? Why?

2.   Given this benefit, why isn't Student Research more widely
     used?

3.   What subject areas do you feel most lend themselves to the
     utilization of Student Research? Why?

4.   Select a subject area *not* named in response to Question #3 and
     tell how you could apply the Student Research approach.

STUDENT TUTORIAL

Definition and Description

Known also as the Lancastrian system, youth-tutoring-youth or monitorial instruction, the Student Tutorial approach utilizes pupils as monitors (tutors) who first learn the lesson from a teacher and then teach small groups or individual students (tutees).

Traditionally the approach has been concerned only with the learning of the tutees. However, the approach also offers a unique learning experience for the student tutors, and this should be considered as a vital portion of the approach.

Advantages or Special Purposes

1. The tutor learns more since teaching is an excellent learning situation.

2. Since the tutor is nearer the age, skill and achievement levels of the tutee than is the teacher, the tutor can better understand the tutee's problems.

3. The Student Tutorial system spreads the talents and knowledge of the teacher.

4. The use of tutors assures all students of individual attention.

5. The Student Tutorial approach provides an economical use of time (in reaching all students).

6. The tutor can develop responsible behavior as well as gain leadership experience.

7. The Student Tutorial system provides a challenging learning experience for the more advanced students in class.

8. Advanced students can often be paired up with remedial students and aid in eliminating troublesome "learning gaps."

9. This is an excellent method to extend the *drill* strategy.

Disadvantages or Limitations

1. Since the tutor and tutees are classmates, tutees often resent being taught by their peers.

2. The tutor is not a teacher and is very limited in instructional skills.

3. Since the tutor usually lacks the teacher's depth of knowledge, the use of tutors may lead to "memorization" transmission only.

4. The use of student tutors removes the teacher from the actual instruction of most of the students.

5. The only feedback the teacher receives is through the tutor and may be distorted.

6. Since the teacher is not present in all of the tutorial sessions, behavior problems are apt to arise.

7. The absence of the teacher from the instructional situation may be a problem of legal liability.

Guidelines for Maximum Utilization

1. All students should be given the opportunity to function as tutors. Remember, all students can learn more by teaching.

2. Use a variety of techniques when instructing the tutors.

3. Aim at the higher cognitive levels in teaching the tutors. It is essential that the tutors have both breadth and depth in the subject.

4. Prepare both the tutors and the tutees as to the role each will play in the tutorial situation.

5. The Student Tutorial approach is excellent to use whenever a large number of students have been absent from class (e.g., flu epidemic). This is usually a dead time, but you can teach those present and use them as tutors when the absent students return to class.

6. When using the tutorial approach, all students should clearly understand the objectives of the lesson. The tutees can tell whether or not they are achieving the objectives, and are thus able to keep you informed.

7. Quick assessment of tutee achievement should be periodically used to provide feedback which will indicate the degree of success of the approach.

8. Unobtrusively observe each of the tutorial situations.

9. Careful pairing of tutor and tutee is necessary to avoid potential personality or discipline problems.

Example

To free the teacher and/or provide a different instructional angle, a good student teaching another student has proved quite successful. This involves the teacher, aide, volunteer parent or student teacher developing lesson plans especially for the pupil needing individual attention. Usually this method is utilized for only short periods of time and on the lower end of the taxonomic scale such as drill (memorization) in multiplication tables, spelling, memorizing poetry or play lines. The adult teacher maintains checks over progress or problems and, of course, is responsible for evaluation.

An interesting approach which has as much, if not more, benefit for the tutor as it does for the tutee is exemplified by a program instituted at Walter T. Moor experimental school in Tallahassee, Florida, in 1970. A group of sixth grade students (who we might describe as "undermotivated" readers) were paired with second graders who were in need of personalized reading instruction---mostly being read to, and being able to read out loud for someone. The sixth graders, who had lost interest in reading, had not lost their need for status, and became very involved, enjoying the admiration they received as the "big teacher." As a consequence, both groups of students showed instant marked improvement which continued throughout the rest of the school year.

Student Tutorial does not give the teacher "more time." No strategy does. A teacher has 60 seconds in every minute just like everyone else. Student Tutorial does, however, allow for a more effective allocation of time. While the teacher must still plan lessons with the tutor (if not for the tutor) he/she does not have to carry them out. This leaves the teacher free to work with small groups or the rest of the class as a whole. "Unplugging" the underachiever from the rest of the class periodically not only gives him/her the chance to receive an academic boost, but also eliminates the potential discipline problems associated with a student-curriculum mismatch.

Summary

The use of students tutoring other students has proven to be a valuable tool for teachers in countless situations. It enables the teacher to provide additional instruction to those pupils having difficulty while continuing to maintain an on-going program with other students in the classroom.

It may be considered a form of *behavior modification* due to the selection process used to designate tutors and tutees. The good student is rewarded by being assigned or appointed as a tutor.

The tutee is rewarded by being selected for additional assistance on the basis of need, acceptable behavior, and a proven desire to want additional help.

Other strategies can play an important part in the Student Tutorial program. They may have only a minor role when used by the tutors but nevertheless are valid points to consider. *Discussion, demonstration, drill, questioning* and *problem solving* are a few of the strategies that enter into the Student Tutorial method.

The mere fact that a peer is aiding the slow student may make the difference between the tutee's success or failure in gaining knowledge and assurance that he/she can do acceptable school work which will enable him/her to be a part of the total classroom learning activities.

Questions to Promote Discussion

1. What do you consider to be the major advantage of the Student Tutorial approach? Why?

2. What do you consider to be the major disadvantage of the Student Tutorial approach? Why?

3. When you weigh the major advantage against the major disadvantage, is the Student Tutorial approach worth using? Why or why not?

4. What could you do to minimize the effects of the major disadvantage of the Student Tutorial approach you listed?

5. In preparing a student to become a tutor what three "pieces of advice" about teaching would you impart?

SYNECTICS

Definition and Description

Synectic exercises encourage greater creativity and allow students to use metaphors, analogies and compressed conflicts to create a paradigm shift in thinking. Alternatives to typical classroom thought processes are allowed to emerge as students begin to use right brain functions. The exercise may be used to make the familiar strange, or to take the familiar and see it in a totally new perspective.

Advantages and Special Purposes

1. Increases creativity in individuals and groups.

2. Works well as a cooperative learning exercise.

3. Encourages community togetherness.

4. Allows divergent thinking processes.

5. Reaches students with different learning styles.

6. Allows for use of imagination and the senses.

7. Useful in problem solving and brainstorming endeavors.

8. Broadens concept attainment.

Disadvantages or Limitations

1. Vocabulary of the model may inhibit students. Terms like synectics, metaphor, analogy and compressed conflict may be imposing at any grade level.

2. The number of steps required to conclude the exercises number as many as 17 procedures and may intimidate a teacher.

3. Students trained in the rigors of left brain concrete sequential thinking may be temporarily stretched out of their comfort zone.

Guidelines for Maximum Utilization

1. Lesson planning time must be spent to carefully develop a flow of the steps to be taken.

2. The teacher must have an eye on time limitations and plan accordingly.

3. Explain the vocabulary of the model and the steps to be taken as they are taken.

4. Be sure to allow for full participation of all students.

5. Have questions and transitions ready in advance to facilitate the flow of the lesson and encourage spontaneity.

6. Encourage openness and creative expression.

7. Accept all responses.

8. Help students stretch their thinking.

9. Be willing to move through a variety of phases depending on the model to be used.

Example of a Model

Phase 1   Describe what we have before us---the present condition.

Phase 2   Suggest direct analogies to the present condition and describe it further.

Phase 3   Let's become the analogy we have selected in Phase 2.

Phase 4   From our discussion in Phases 2 and 3 let us suggest severa compressed conflicts and choose one.

Phase 5   Allow the compressed conflict to inspire yet another analogy.

Phase 6   Move back to the original task or problem and use the las analogy or the entire experience to proceed with a new mindset

Summary

Synectic exercises can be used to develop creative thinking o creative writing skills, explore social problems, or solve problems. The exercises lead to concept attainment, expanding concepts and to discovery and invention. The process encourages group cohesion and generate: energy in the classroom. Shared experience fosters interpersona understanding and community spirit.

Questions to Promote Discussion

1.   At what age is it reasonable to expect elementary schoo students to be able to think in terms of metaphor and analogies:

2.   Should creative thought process be taught as part of the regula school curriculum? Why or why not?

3. Are teachers intruding on the personal growth of students if they ask them to relate their feelings and sensate experience in class?

4. What do you consider to be the best use of the synectic exercise?

TEAM TEACHING

Definition and Description

Team Teaching is an arrangement in which two or more teachers cooperatively plan, teach, and evaluate a group of students. Teaching teams may also include student teachers and/or paraprofessional personnel.

Teams may be organized on a departmental basis, an inter-departmental or interdisciplinary pattern, or on a grade level basis. Most Team Teaching arrangements include instruction in large groups, small groups and individual study.

As such, the various strategies throughout this book are applicable to the Team Teaching arrangement. However, the peculiarities of the arrangement itself require that certain dimensions or parameters be considered.

Advantages or Special Purposes

1. Team Teaching capitalizes upon the special competencies, talents, and interests of each teacher.

2. Joint planning, teaching and evaluation by the team members stimulates the professional growth of the teachers involved.

3. Students may be grouped on an educational basis rather than an administrative basis.

4. Students will be exposed to several teachers with different backgrounds and approaches, thus providing an enriching experience.

5. The use of small groups and individualized study provides for individual student needs.

6. Large group presentations make possible more efficient use of time and resources (such as visiting speakers).

7. Teaching teams benefit the team members; beginning teachers are helped by experienced teachers. The more experienced gather up-to-date information and ideas from the enthusiastic newcomers.

8. The use of large groups, small groups, and individual study conducted by various team members provides more interesting and less monotonous routines in the area of traditional strategies.

9. Teachers get more help from the non-instructional personnel of the school such as the counselor, librarian, or media specialist.

10. Teachers have more time for planning, preparation and follow-up.

11. Team Teaching may be used for all or a part of the students' day.

12. Team Teaching also adds flexibility to the school curriculum and daily schedule.

Disadvantages or Limitations

1. Team Teaching calls for special physical facilities to provide for large group-small group arrangements.

2. The cost per student of effective Team Teaching is often higher than for more traditional approaches.

3. Team Teaching is attractive and seems simple, but its actual application is more complex for administrators as well as teachers.

4. Teaching efficiency can be reduced by personality and professional conflicts among the team members.

5. Specialization on the part of the teachers may be carried to the point that the student loses sight of the whole subject or teaching/learning goals.

6. Large groups and a myriad of teachers may only confuse and alienate the student.

7. Team Teaching may in actuality be meeting the needs of teachers rather than those of the students.

8. The scheduling of large groups, small groups, and individual study is often extremely complicated and difficult to communicate without misunderstanding.

Guidelines for Maximum Utilization

1. Team Teaching requires understanding and acceptance by the administration and parents as well as the teachers involved.

2. Team members selected should be those who possess the needed personal qualities for cooperation as well as instructional competence.

3. Adopt Team Teaching on an experimental or trial basis at first.

4. State the objectives of the experiment and design the evaluation procedure in advance of its use.

5. In the planning sessions define the roles to be played by each team member. If a team leader is to be named, determine selection processes and job responsibilities prior to utilizing this strategy.

6. Provide time and resources for the team members to prepare thoroughly.

7. Large group activity is most appropriate to introduce a new topic or unit, to summarize or conclude a unit, and to provide information beneficial for the entire class.

8. Small groups may be best used to discuss large group presentations and topics of student interest.

9. Individual study may help students pursue areas of individual need and interest and develop the skills associated with individual inquiry.

10. Further utilization of Team Teaching should be undertaken only if the experimental attempt proves extremely satisfactory to all parties concerned (students, teachers, parents, administrators, board of education, etc.).

Summary

Besides scheduling and material arrangement the most important facet of Team Teaching is the personalities of the teachers involved. It is paramount to the success of this strategy that the teachers involved like each other, cooperate, and communicate openly and honestly. All the finest materials, plans and facilities will not make Team Teaching work if the teachers cannot work together.

In the area of communication, it is vitally important to student progress for teachers to case manage daily on learner needs, problems and achievements and to plan assistance or promotion for those areas.

Questions to Promote Discussion

1. What do you consider to be the major strength of Team Teaching? Why?

2. In the 1960s Team Teaching was the "in" thing. However, it alleged potential was never realized. What factors do you fee retarded this development? Why?

3. What is the most significant factor in the proper use of Team Teaching? Why?

4. What would you do if you were part of a teaching team and another member always wanted to be "in charge?"

VALUE CLARIFICATION

Definition and Description

Value Clarification is a process-oriented instructional method which has one or more of the following purposes:

a) To teach students that a particular value object should have a predetermined rating;

b) To assist students in making the most rationally defensible value judgment they can make about a value object in question;

c) To instill in students the ability and inclination to make rationally defensible value judgments; and/or

d) To teach students how to function as group members who are attempting to come to a common value judgment about a particular value object. (NCSS, p. 18)

Example

Purpose A - Teaching specific citizenship attributes as desirable; teaching that socialized medicine is detrimental; teaching that polygamy is evil; teaching that the United States is the best country.

Purposes B and C - Students are taught the following rational mental functions: 1) The proposed facts supporting a value judgment must be true or well confirmed; 2) the facts must be genuinely relevant; 3) other things being equal, the greater the range of relevant facts included in making the judgment, the more adequate the judgment will be; and, 4) the value principle implied by the judgment must be agreeable to the person involved in making the judgment. (NCSS, p. 18) (Purpose B is concerned with these four processes in regard to a specific value object; Purpose C is concerned with establishing a general mind-set in the student with which to make future value judgments.)

Purpose D - This purpose is centered around teaching students methods for resolving value conflicts. Six steps are involved: 1) Reducing differences in the interpretation of the value question;

2) Reducing differences in the purported facts assembled; 3) reducing differences in the assessed truth of purported facts; 4) reducing differences in the relevance of facts; 5) reducing differences in the tentative value judgments; and, 6) reducing differences in testing the acceptability of value principles. (NCSS, p.122)

As can be seen by the above descriptions, Value Clarification is a complex and multifaceted instructional strategy. The most prevalent purpose is A, that of instilling a predetermined value judgement about a value object. It is also, interestingly enough, the most rejected purpose by most of today's authorities in values clarification. The major reasons for this rejection range from accusations of indoctrination to those of stunting rational thought processes in students. Any person going through graduate school is familiar with the political necessity of sometimes espousing a particularly non-heartfelt set of values. The repugnance of such unenlightened teachings (better known as "indoctrination") is the reason why Purpose A is ignored for the rest of this chapter.

Advantages or Special Purposes

1. A person who works to clarify values:
    a) Establishes a more purposeful direction in his or her life, thereby increasing personal and professional productivity;
    b) Has more consideration for fellow humans;
    c) Is more reliable because he/she makes clear where he/she stands;
    d) Gradually becomes more aware and discerning;
    e) Learns to make honest and considered choices;
    f) Is less affected by outside pressures and prejudices;
    g) Makes more solid and defensible decisions; and,
    h) Achieves more consistency between self-I-am and self-I-want-to-be.

2. A group that works to clarify values:
    a) Illustrates to members that others have similar problems
    b) Gives individuals peer feedback and alternative solutions

      c)   Establishes group solidarity and mutual trust; and,
      d)   Helps develop leadership potential in members.

3.   The teacher gains valuable insight into the real needs and interests of students.

4.   The teacher becomes more aware of the attitudes, values, beliefs, and motivating forces behind student thought and behavior.

5.   Subject matter can be made more personally relevant when combined with Value Clarification exercises.

Disadvantages or Limitations

1.   It takes most teachers a number of months to become adept at conducting successful Value Clarification sessions.

2.   The temptation for the teacher to "moralize" (a definite taboo!) is almost overpowering.

3.   Sessions, although potentially·valuable, are time consuming.

4.   An insensitive teacher could allow students to get emotionally "bruised" if conflicts that arise cannot be healthfully resolved.

5.   Some students tend to dominate discussion, while others will take a "wallflower" role.

6.   It is impractical (as well as undesirable) to evaluate in terms of establishing a letter or percentage grade for Value Clarification exercises.

Guidelines for Maximum Utilization

1. According to Simon and Clark, the Values Clarification process is
    basically as follows:

    Choosing ---
    a. Lasting values must be freely chosen.
    b. Values must be chosen from among alternatives.
    c. There must be thoughtful consideration of the consequences of
        each alternative.

    Prizing ---
    d. The value must be prized and cherished.
    e. Development of a willingness to publicly proclaim the value
        chosen.

    Acting ---
    f. The zenith of values clarification is acting on values.
    g. True values will be acted upon repeatedly. (Simon, p.35 & 55)

    These seven steps of the process should be kept in mind when
    reviewing the guidelines.

2. An atmosphere of trust is essential. Never use students' words
    against them or as a means of "rational embarrassment."

3. It is essential for the teacher to be a member of the group,
    rather than an aloof or authoritarian observer. Therefore, the
    instructor should make, "I feel...," "I believe..." statements just
    as involved students are expected to do. Students will reveal
    to the teacher (and group) in direct proportion to the teacher's
    revelations.

4. The four steps (Simon, p.55) in the Values Clarification
    strategy include:

    a) *Build a climate of trust and comfort-caring.* This is a process
        of making everyone feel at home. Is everyone aware of where

the restroom and water fountains are? Is everyone comfortable? Does everyone know what is going to happen and why? This helps establish the atmosphere of trust and concern for group members so necessary to productive sessions.

b) *Begin with easy to answer questions and non-threatening activities.* This activity includes questions easily answered in public. This beginning procedure recognizes true values which must be willingly displayed publicly. Some sample non-threatening ice-breakers:

    i)   How many feel that health food is better than typical supermarket offerings?
    ii)   What's wrong with being "just a housewife?"
    iii)   Should retirement be mandatory?
    iv)   Should teenagers get an allowance? Etc.

(Questions, of course, should be tailored to the social or age group involved.)

Attempts at clarification should be made even at this early stage by asking such questions as:

    i)   Does/should everyone feel this way?
    ii)   What could be some possible results of this action?
    iii)   Anyone have a different idea on this topic?
    iv)   Could anyone defend the opposite point of view?

c) *Gradually probe deeper.* Before deeper questioning can take place, the leader and the group *must* feel at ease with each other. Likewise, the leader must feel at ease with the questions being utilized. Some examples:

    i)   How do people act on what they value?
    ii)   How should we treat people who act on values not. generally accepted by society?
    iii)   Do groups have group values? Some examples?
    iv)   How do you feel about the way you act on your values?
    v)   What values, if any, should be universally mandated?

d) *Issuing a challenge to action.* The most difficult part of the Values Clarification process is challenging to action. True, it is up to the student to choose when and how to act upon his/her values, but it is up to the group leader (teacher) to offer alternatives and challenge with questions *with gentle discretion*

i)   So, you believe in respecting your elders---how are you going to act on this in the next week?

ii)   If you believe that health is important, what steps are you taking to preserve your own?

iii) If you feel that education is so important, how do you plan to illustrate this in your own life.

iv)   If helping others is, as you say, one of the major human purposes, how do you plan to exhibit this in your life?

v)   If you believe lying is sometimes necessary, what kind of personal guidelines need to be established to determine when to lie and when it is inappropriate?

vi)   If you believe that charity is important, when are you going to help collect donations for your favorite charity

A wrap-up to each values clarification session in terms of "What have we learned today?" questions is helpful in solidifying personal revelations and decisions. It also provides a sense of real accomplishment providing positive carry-over motivation for the next session.

Summary

Proponents of Values Clarification feel that it is a long overdue and vital part of education. They hope it will send forth a generation of truth-seekers who are strong in their honesty with themselves as well as with their peers. Some educators believe it is mere fad and doesn't "put the-money-in-the-bank" as an educational and human investment compared to solid subject-matter teaching. Others, like the authors of this book, see a new potential in linking values clarification with subject matter to make a more personally relevant and meaningful curriculum than ever before possible. It appears to be the ideal approach to the "internalizing of subject-matter" problem we educators have been plagued with for centuries. We urge more investigatory projects in this area.

Questions to Promote Discussion

1. What do you consider to be the major benefit of the Values Clarification process in education? Why?

2. How could a teacher take precautions to prevent participants from becoming "emotionally bruised" during the Values Clarification process?

3. How would you defend the use of Values Clarification in your classroom?

4. What are the advantages and disadvantages of instilling specific values in students?

Part Two

TEACHING SUB-STRATEGIES

Any medium that enhances the effectiveness of a teaching strategy

TEACHING TECHNIQUES WITH MEDIA

Have you ever noticed that the fancier restaurant meals have more garnishes, the expensive cars more options, and the elite apartments all those nice electronic extras? Many times it's those "extras" that really *make* the meal, car, or apartment. Unsurprisingly, the same principle applies to a lesson being taught. While some teachers regard media as superfluous, the expert teacher recognizes the tremendous enhancement of lesson impact afforded by proper use of sub-strategies. It can, and often does, make the difference between a lesson that flies and one that fails.

There are some general principles to keep in mind that, if adhered to, improve sub-strategy selection and utilization processes.

1. No one medium is the best for all purposes.

2. Sub-strategy use should be consistent with teaching objectives.

3. Teachers must be familiar with media content - how they may be used most advantageously, the difficulty level in relationship to student competency, conditions of availability, and suitability to class size (large group, small group, individual study).

4. The sub-strategy must fit student capabilities and learning styles.

5. A sub-strategy should be selected objectively rather than on the basis of personal bias.

6. The physical environment significantly affects the results obtained with media. (Brown, p.71)

Procedures

The basic five-step utilization formula that has been used for decade
is still a good one. It is the sub-strategy equivalent of strategy lesson
planning.

1. *Prepare Yourself*
   Prior to the lesson, listen to the record, preview the film
   filmstrip, video tape, or picture set. Develop your "plan" with
   introductory comments, questions, evaluation items, etc.

2. *Prepare Environment*
   Arrange equipment and materials. Arrange chairs, desks, tables
   lighting. Make sure ventilation and room temperature are
   comfortable.

3. *Prepare Class*
   Introduce the sub-strategy item, explain objectives, stress what
   is to be watched/listened for, and what learners will be expected
   to do with the information gained (discussion, test, enjoyment
   only, etc.)

4. *Presentation*
   Performance of sub-strategy should be done with proper
   equipment or material operation (focus film, adjust sound, etc.)

5. *Follow Up*
   Summarize, review, discuss, question, test or whatever plan
   were made to help "solidify" the experience. (Brown, p.67)

This five-step procedure is a fundamental one. It is not sacred, and the
teacher should feel creatively free to experiment with variations. An
example variation might be just showing a film without any guidelines of
introduction, in order to get the students' uncolored impressions. A
display of still photos on poverty can have a message with no
introduction or follow-up. In other words, as is the case with most
guidelines, they are meant to guide and suggest and not to provide
restrictions.

ub-Strategies Explained

Each sub-strategy is presented with a brief *description, advantages r special purposes, disadvantages or limitations,* and general *application* atements. Again, these are general statements meant to familiarize and uide, and are not intended as iron-clad rules. Most teachers will be urprised to discover just how many sub-strategies are available for ddition to their professional arsenal of teaching techniques.

AUDIO RECORDINGS

Description

Audio Recordings include tapes (reel-to-reel, cassette, cards), record (disc recordings) and compact discs. Tapes can be teacher-recorded student-recorded, or purchased pre-recorded from numerous companies The fastest growing aspects of the educational media industry are that c pre-recorded cassettes, usually packaged with visuals and/or programmed text and the multimedia computer with compact disc an onscreen text. Equipment for playing audio recordings can be purchase at minimal cost and is operated easily by the youngest of students. Dis recordings and tapes are now found in most school and public librarie

Advantages or Special Purposes

1. Audio materials are the natural tools for teaching and improvin listening skills.

2. Audio materials have high versatility and ease of operation fc their relatively low cost.

3. Storage problems are minimal.

4. Material that is recorded can be absorbed faster than the printe word.

5. Recordings can be used by small groups, large groups, c individuals (and with earphones can be utilized by individual in the midst of a group).

6. Foreign languages and speech skills are probably best taught b regular supplemental work with audio materials.

7. In elementary schools, individualized audio work not only help tailor curriculum to specific student needs, but it also helps

minimize distractions (children with headphones on are psychologically isolated as well as being on a short tether!).

Disadvantages or Limitations

1. Teachers may have a tendency to overuse recordings and bore students.

2. Although costs are moderate, they may still be prohibitive for programs with small budgets.

Application

1. Plan by establishing objectives *and then* acquiring the appropriate recordings.

2. Preview material and prepare an outline on the important points. Decide what you will do to introduce, discuss, and evaluate the recording(s).

3. Motivate students to listen by explaining objectives and evaluation criteria.

4. Start material only after making sure everyone is alert to purposes and is comfortable.

5. Follow-up the lesson with discussion, questions, and suggestions. Go over evaluation aspects again if students are to be tested at a later date.

6. Some suggestions for different uses of audio media:

   a) Utilize pre-recorded and print materials in conjunction with *learning centers.*
   b) People involved in speech, drama, teaching, ministerial work, singing, politics, and radio-television broadcasting

should be required periodically to furnish their instructor with tapes of their rehearsed speaking abilities.

c)   Allow individual students or small groups to make taped presentations on special projects.

d)   Have individual students who have special hobbies, areas of expertise, or unique experiences make an audio *learning packet* that can become a permanently available resource in the classroom.

e)   Have students make tapes of interviews (see *interview* strategy) of community persons, visiting celebrities, or local hobbyists.

f)   Record popular music from the radio and utilize in discussion of "what pop music is saying to us today."

g)   Have students tape their version of a radio show on a specific topic.

7.   Keep equipment and disc recordings in good shape by regular maintenance. Problems can be reduced by training students to use the media properly in the first place.

8.   Set up a code system for classifying and cataloging your recordings and set aside a permanent storage/display area for them.

BOOKS

Textbooks and other books are often overlooked as media. However, they do communicate to the student and are subject to certain inherent qualities as are other sub-strategies.

Advantages or Special Purposes

1. The information is permanent and usually well written.

2. Proper material is available for almost any reading level.

3. Books are reusable.

4. The learner controls the pace at which the material is received.

5. Books use color and appeal to the visual sense.

6. Books can be used to meet objectives of both cognitive and affective domains.

Disadvantages or Limitations

1. Books can be expensive to use.

2. Motion, if required, cannot be shown.

3. Some other instructional strategy must be utilized to make the information available to a group.

4. Many students do not know how to "use" a book to achieve maximum benefit.

5. The motivation to read is often lacking in students.

6. All of the information a teacher desires to portray throug
    books is rarely located concisely in one book, and usually mus
    be pieced together from several sources.

Application

1. Occasionally spend time helping students learn how to get th
    most out of a book.

2. Clarify the purpose, or purposes, to be served by reading fror
    a given book.

3. Focus on problems which may require portions of several book
    to be read in order to solve the problem.

4. First, emphasize concepts in having students report on readin;
    Then have them present data or details which demonstrate th
    concepts.

5. Utilize teaching strategies which enable the learners to appl
    the information read in the book.

BULLETIN BOARDS

Description

Bulletin boards are either stationary or portable (the latter being handy as room dividers). Most are faced with cork, facilitating the attachment of display items. They are often utilized for long-term (more than a few days) display of concepts being emphasized in class.

Advantages or Special Purposes

1.   Bulletin boards can be used to stimulate student interest in specified topics of study.

2.   Students can be motivated in an area of study by having them participate in constructing a bulletin board display.

3.   As austere in decor as many classrooms are, bulletin boards provide an opportunity for increasing environmental attractiveness through colorful and eye-pleasing displays.

4.   When only one copy of a map, newspaper clippings, or a chart is available, bulletin board placement allows a number of students to study it at the same time.

5.   Group projects or reports can be displayed effectively.

6.   Individual student interests, hobbies, photographs, etc. can be exhibited.

Disadvantages or Limitations

1. Bulletin boards in public schools are an excellent source of sharp objects for posterior impalement.

2. The constant need to do bulletin board face-lifting can be an extensive bit of busy work for teachers.

3. Good bulletin board preparation takes planning and time.

4. A poorly done bulletin board makes a room unattractive.

5. If the board is used to display only excellent students' excellent works, it acts as a constant reminder to the less able student of his/her shortcomings.

Application

1. Planning is essential for successful bulletin boards.
    a)   Know what idea or concept you wish to impart.
    b)   Plan the display by first making a sketch and list of materials needed.
    c)   Involve students by assigning various responsibilities, including acquiring and shaping materials and actual construction of the display.
    d)   Be creative in use of materials, colors and textures.

2. Make student involvement an enjoyable learning experience rather than an "assignment."

3. Take class time to discuss the finished product and its implications.

4. Change bulletin boards frequently, approximately every two weeks.

CHALKBOARD

Description

Historically, teachers could have any color of chalkboard they wanted as long as it was black. Today the chalkboard comes in all colors, shapes, sizes and degrees of portability. Some have special surfaces that require a particular type of felt-tip pen rather than chalk. Most times, however, this medium includes a large writing area, a writing substance (usually chalk), and an eraser.

The chalkboard is so common that not much attention is paid to maximizing the use of this fantastic sub-strategy, but by following the guidelines below, the potential of even the trusty old "blackboard" can be greatly increased.

Advantages or Special Purposes

1. Availability. Most areas assigned for instruction are equipped with chalkboards. Also, if more board space is needed, portable boards of various types and styles are handy.

2. The chalkboard is inexpensive, especially when the usable life of the board is considered.

3. It is flexible in use in the sense that teachers may use it, students may use it and changes can be easily made through erasure.

4. Space. Lots of writing space is usually provided.

5. The chalkboard can be used to present more formally prepared lessons, or for informal, spontaneous sessions.

6. Ideas can be dealt with at all levels from facts to concepts, from cognitive to affective learning.

7. Various colored chalk or pens can be used to develop the topic, show parts or build associations.

8. A point-by-point outline of a presentation can be made on the spot with diagrams, charts, and other accentuation drawn at the appropriate moment.

9. The visual communication of the chalkboard directs attention of the class to the purposes of the lecture or discussion.

10. Ideas or topics suggested in discussion can be listed on the board, reorganized, deleted, added to, and put in final form.

11. Test or discussion questions can be put on the board and covered up before the class assembles, then revealed at the appropriate time. This can save on time and cost of duplication materials.

12. A number of students can do practice or drill work on the board at one time, allowing the instructor to give feedback immediately.

Disadvantages or Limitations

1. The chalkboard carries with it a "temporariness." Material put on the board cannot be saved or made permanent.

2. Chalkboards are often fixed in such a way that they are "too low for the teacher to use and too high for the kids to use," i.e. they are not always at a comfortable height for all potential users.

3. Being fixed, chalkboards can put restrictions on the use of classroom space and classroom activities as students need to be placed where they can see the boards.

4. Problems can arise for students who have vision impairments.

5. With age, use of certain types of chalk, and/or improper cleaning practices, boards can become "cloudy" as they retain chalk dust.

6. Some teachers are psyched-out of using the board because they feel a lack of artistic ability.

7. Motion cannot be easily shown.

8. A teacher's handwriting or spelling deficiencies are most obvious when using the chalkboard.

9. Making use of the chalkboard necessitates turning one's back on the class, which can allow disruption (and can also be dangerous in some of today's schools).

10. Chalkboard work can be messy.

11. Writing on the board can be "down time" and may break the class's train of thought and/or discussion.

Application

1. Be prepared. See that the chalkboard and erasers are properly cleaned and maintained. Ensure that chalk is available in sufficient quantity; students get very tired of watching teachers search constantly during class for a piece of chalk (or eraser).

2. Plan what you are going to write on the board: a) keep writing to a minimum by using key words or conceptual diagrams; and b) develop topics by using the board from left to right and top to bottom.

3. Keep writing a) neat, b) large, heavy and high enough to be visible by all, c) brief; and d) specific.

4. Practice writing and/or printing in a straight line.

5. Use yellow chalk on a green board, white on a black board, etc

6. If your chalk squeaks, simply break the piece in half.

7. Learn to stand so you do not block the view of students as you use the board.

8. Avoid writing and "talking into" the board at the same time.

9. Put the chalk down when you are through writing. This reduces the chances for distraction caused by playing with the chalk.

10. Use the eraser to remove errors or make changes. Using your hands only smears the chalk and may deposit oil on the board, which can serve as a dust collector.

11. In erasing the board, use a down-sweep erasing motion. Erasing the board with a side-to-side motion only enables the students to observe (from a most unflattering angle) the teacher doing something resembling the "Twist." It also causes chalk-dust particles to fly into the air instead of into the collector tray

12. When you are through with the material, erase it completely so that it will not serve as a distraction while the next topic is being considered.

13. Intersperse writing on the board with questions or verbal emphasis. Keep the class aware of what is being put on the board and why.

14. If important drawings or maps are needed on the board, a teacher is wise to save time by 1) doing them before class, and 2) copying a projection on the board (from a filmstrip, slide, or opaque projector) rather than "free-handing" it.

15. Chalkboard etiquette: If someone will be using the board after you, please don't leave it for him/her to erase. It's nice to clean the eraser against the board as well.

CHARTS

Description

Any pre-prepared graphic device or poster can be used as a chart. It can consist of drawings, graphs, words, pictures, cut-outs, etc.

Advantages or Special Purposes

1. Charts are permanent and reusable.

2. Charts are portable.

3. Charts can be used for ideas ranging from the simple to the complex.

4. They can be used alone to deal with a single concept or as a part of a series of several charts in developing a theme.

5. They appeal to the visual sense of students.

6. Charts can utilize color to indicate steps of development.

7. Students can make charts to show their understanding of the subject.

Disadvantages or Limitations

1. Charts are often too complicated or too detailed to be useful.

2. Students with vision impairments may have difficulty seeing.

3. Motion cannot be shown.

4. Teachers may feel they lack the artistic ability to prepare charts.

5. Charts that are big enough to be seen may be cumbersome to handle.

6. As information changes, charts can become outdated.

7. Professionally-prepared charts can be costly.

Application

1. Plan well so that the chart fits the lesson.

2. Make sure the elements of the chart are large, neat, clear, and vivid enough to be seen.

3. Use a minimum of elements on the chart---avoid crowding.

4. Use color when it will help explain the material.

5. Avoid blocking the learner's view.

6. Use a pointer so that you will be showing the total chart when identifying only a portion of it.

7. Affix the chart to the wall, an easel, etc., so that you will not need to hold it. This will also ensure that the chart is steady for viewing.

8. Computer technology can aide in the preparation of "professional" looking charts either on-screen or printed out.

CHART PAD

Description

The chart pad is a large tablet attached to an easel. It is written on with a felt-tipped marker, grease pencil, or crayon.

Advantages or Special Purposes

1. Material written on a chart pad page can be retained for later review.

2. The chart pad can be prepared in advance

3. Written material on the chart pad can be used by simply removing the page from the pad and attaching it somewhere in the room.

4. After a lesson, chart pad pages can be stored and used the next time the lesson is to be taught.

5. The chart pad and easel are light-weight and portable and can be used where board space is limited or unavailable.

6. Various colors can be used in developing the topic, which can be useful in showing steps, sequences, etc.

7. Students can use the chart pad.

8. It appeals to the visual sense of students.

Disadvantages or Limitations

1. Only a small writing space is available.

2.   Chart pads cannot be erased and "scribbling out" is a distraction.

3.   Students with vision problems may not be able to see.

4.   Motion cannot easily be shown.

5.   The cost (over that of an already available chalkboard, for example) can be prohibitive for some tightly-budgeted systems.

Application

1.   It is essential to plan in advance what you are going to write.

2.   Write *only* key words or make conceptual diagrams.

3.   Avoid writing and "talking into" the chart pad at the same time.

4.   Be careful not block the learners' view.

5.   Use color when it will help explain the material.

6.   Write legibly - large, neat and vivid.

7.   Either turn over or remove the page when you are finished with it, so that it will not serve as a distraction.

8.   Chart pads are great for brainstorming sessions where sheets can be taped up for scrutinizing and processing.

COMPUTER

[This chapter was graciously prepared by Denise Leong, Asst. Prof.,
Marian College, Fond du Lac, Wisconsin]

Description

A computer is a machine that can input, process, manipulate, store, and output information according to instructions provided by a program stored on computer software. Software is available for such things as word processing, problem solving, tutorials, graphics, and multimedia presentations.

The basic computer configuration includes a keyboard (input), the central processing unit (CPU), a disk drive (storage), and a monitor (output). Presentation devices, such as the liquid crystal display (LCD) panel, provide enlarged images for group viewing. Peripheral devices, which can enhance the basic input and output of the computer, include printers, scanners, modems, CD-ROM drives, and videodisc players.

There are many different types of printers - dot-matrix, inkjet, and laser---which vary in speed and quality of the printouts. Color is available on the more expensive printers, and most all are capable of producing graphics.

A scanner enables one to convert an image on a page into a computer graphic. With an optical character reader (OCR), one can scan words and convert them into word processing text. In both cases, the converted material can then be manipulated and stored by the computer.

A modem (modulator/demodulator) translates information so that it can be transmitted from one computer to another computer over ordinary telephone lines. With modems, computer users are able to communicate worldwide where phone access is available. Telecommunication applications include electronic mail services, bulletin boards, research, and electronic conferencing.

CD-ROM drives and videodisc players are used with CD-ROM's (compact disk read only memory) and videodiscs---mediums that store huge amounts of audio and visual material. For instance, CD-ROM's can hold over 600 megabytes of information, over four hundred times as much as a 3.5" floppy disk, while videodiscs can hold over 100,000 still images.

Advantages or Special Purposes

1. Students are highly motivated to use computers.

2. Computers can provide help in remediation as well as challenges for advanced study.

3. Work can be done collaboratively.

4. Pacing can be individualized.

5. Programs can compile records of each student's progress.

6. Computers are geared for visual, auditory, and kinesthetic learners.

7. The color, animation, and sound of programs are extremely stimulating for students.

8. Computers provide an exciting alternative to lecture, basals, and workbooks.

9. Computers can be integrated throughout curriculum as a means to access information, hypothesize, create, explore, and present knowledge.

10. Telecommunications provide global access and promote global awareness

11. Computers can foster creativity.

12.   Computers are just plain fun.

Advantages for Use as a Word Processor

1.   Revisions are easily done. Students will <u>want</u> to revise.

2.   Pride in professional printouts, especially for students
     with poor handwriting

3.   Mundane mechanical skills, such as spelling, can be checked by
     computer programs with reinforcement lessons provided to the
     student.

Disadvantages or Limitations

1.   Technology is expensive.

2.   Students can become overstimulated by computer activities.

3.   Noise increases proportionately to the students' enjoyment.

4.   Planning time in daily schedules to include computer use can
     be difficult.

5.   Careful planning for manipulating time and activities will be
     needed in case of shortages of equipment, software, space, etc.

6.   Mechanical problems will occur just when you don't need
     them.   (Murphy's Computer Law)

7.   Teachers may not have the training to feel comfortable with
     technology.

8.   Software for whole classroom use is expensive.

9. Some students will view the computer as a toy and not use it consciously.

10. Primary students will be slow in their keyboarding. Intermediate students will need to learn keyboarding.

Applications

1. Demonstration of the part of the program to be covered that day should be done in a whole group setting, away from the computers. Handouts containing keystrokes and procedures should be given to students to follow along.

2. Assign seats for computer setting <u>before</u> students move to computers.

3. Use the rule "Ask three before you ask me." Students should not depend on you alone for help---you cannot be in 25 places at once! If a student asks three other students, and they don't know the answer either, then all four should signal for help. Those four are now your "helpers!"

4. Have "HELP" cards for students to place on top of their monitors when they need you. This avoids having 50 hands waving in the air above screams of, "Help me!"

5. Always have a backup assignment for the students who finish early or to keep them busy while you are helping others or fixing the inevitable breakdowns.

6. Wear comfortable shoes that enable you to chase from one side of the room to another in 2 seconds flat.

7. If you need everyone's attention, make sure all hands are off the keyboards and eyes are on you.

8. Keep students aware of time. Allow five minutes for saving and shut down of computers.

9. Format disks yourself, or purchase preformatted disks. Have a disk for each student with names written on the label. Keep disks stored in your room.

10. Printers are sensitive, and paper jams can occur easily. For elementary students, either assign one reliable, coordinated student as "rip-off" person, or establish yourself as the only one authorized to remove printouts from printers.

CUTAWAYS

A cutaway is designed to show the learner the "insides" of the object. The cutaway might simply be the real thing with part of the "skin" removed. Or, it might be on the order of a scaled-up or scaled-down model, depending on what needs to be seen. Human anatomical models are examples of cutaways.

Advantages or Special Purposes

Cutaways have all of the advantages of *realia* (see page 266) plus the following:

1. The student can observe the "insides" of the object, which are normally hidden from view.

2. The actual operational activities can be observed and analyzed.

3. Cutaways may be purchased commercially.

4. Cutaways may be home-made by the teacher and/or the students.

5. Cutaways may be reduced in size or enlarged in size for easier study.

6. Cutaways come in working and non-working styles.

Disadvantages or Limitations

The same disadvantages apply to the cutaways as to the use of *realia*, plus the following:

1. Cutaways can be costly when purchased.

2. Cutaways can be time consuming for the teacher and the learners when they are home-made.

3. Because cutaways are often larger or smaller than the real object, students may misinterpret the actual size.

Application

Cutaways are used in the same manner as *realia*, plus the following guidelines:

1. Be sure the cutaway emphasizes that which the learner should observe.

2. Use working cutaways when motion is essential.

3. Relate the cutaway to the true size of the real object.

4. Allow students to make cutaways when possible.

FILMSTRIPS

Description

Filmstrips are made up of a series of still pictures placed in sequential order on 35mm film. Each individual picture is called a "frame." Filmstrips are usually between twelve and fifty frames in length.

Advantages or Special Purposes

1. A wide variety of commercially-produced filmstrips is available.

2. The generally high production quality of filmstrips provides visual stimulation and motivates the learner.

3. Filmstrips are easily stored. A "mountain of knowledge" can be stored in a small container.

4. Filmstrip projectors are generally available to the teacher and are easy to operate.

5. Students can use the filmstrip projector in making student presentations.

6. Pictures, diagrams, drawings, and charts can all be utilized on filmstrips.

Disadvantages or Limitations

1. Home-made filmstrips are hard to make; thus the teacher generally has to rely upon commercially produced strips.

2. Commercially-produced filmstrips "structure" the lesson for the teacher.

3. Filmstrips are inflexible in making the presentation.

4. The "outdating" of a significant number of frames causes the entire filmstrip to become obsolete.

5. Commercially produced filmstrips do not always turn out to be exactly as described in the brochures.

6. The room must be darkened, affecting both teacher control and meaningful student discussion.

7. In a darkened room, it is difficult for the teacher to read a script should one be included with the filmstrip.

8. Students cannot easily take notes in the dark.

9. Filmstrips do not show motion.

Application

1. Preview the filmstrip to be sure it is in line with your objectives.

2. Rehearse the presentation to ensure that you have enough time, you are thoroughly familiar with the material, the machine is working properly and all physical arrangements are acceptable.

3. Keep the room lights on and projector lights off during the introduction of the filmstrip. The same applies to the summary discussion after the viewing period.

4. Any specifics which you expect students to retain should be reviewed.

FLANNEL BOARD-MAGNETIC BOARD

Description

Flannel board, flannel graph, hook and eye board are all names given to a device in which certain fabric is stretched over a board or frame. Cut-outs, backed by a compatible material which causes the cut-outs to cling to the fabric, are placed on the board to develop the lesson.

Magnetic boards are also used in the same manner as flannel boards. Cutouts with magnatized backs are used on a metallic surface.

Advantages or Special Purposes

1. These boards are best used in lessons requiring a step-by-step presentation.

2. The cut-outs can be moved, rearranged or removed to show action or the results of action and changes in the relationship of the subject material.

3. Visualization capabilities enhance a verbal presentation.

4. Judicious use of color attracts the attention of the learner.

5. These aids can be light-weight and portable or they can be permanently fixed.

6. Cut-outs are relatively easy for the teacher to construct.

7. Students can make cut-outs and use the boards.

Disadvantages or Limitations

1. Small cut-outs cannot be easily seen.

2. Cut-outs can be easily lost.

3. The flannel board has for so long been used predominantly with younger children that it may seem "childish" to older learners.

4. Less spontaneity is afforded since the prepared cut-outs limit what is considered.

5. Space is usually limited.

Application

1. The lesson must be rehearsed in advance and all materials organized accordingly for use.

2. Be sure all materials are present at the time they will be needed.

3. Use color in a systematic way if it will help show the sequence of important data.

4. Do not block the view of the students.

5. Avoid "talking into" the board.

6. Involve students in making cut-outs.

7. Encourage students to show their understanding by having them use the board.

GRAPHS

Graphs are holistic representations of numerical relationships. The three types commonly used are the line graph, bar graph, and pie graph.

a) *Line Graphs* - The line graph is the only one of the three types that represents two dimensions of measurement, one on the vertical axis and one on the horizontal. Each point on the graph represents a value in both dimensions.

b) *Bar Graph* - A bar graph can either compare the relative size of several items or the parts of a whole in relation to that whole.

c) *Pie Graph* - Pie graphs are reserved almost solely for showing the parts of a whole in relationship to each other. A common example is the "healthy diet concept," showing the percentage of dairy products, meat, vegetables, sea food, grains, and fruit that should be consumed for optimal health.

Advantages or Special Purposes

1. Mathematical or proportional relationships in sets of data can be quickly and accurately perceived by the viewer.

2. A graph can be constructed with very little effort and/or artistic talent.

3. Graphs can be done in different colors or shadings to include a third dimension or quality.

Disadvantages or Limitations

1. Care must be taken that pictorial representation doesn
   oversimplify and, therefore, inaccurately depict complex data

2. Planning and preparation take time and special materials suc
   as graph paper, colored pens, straightedge, posterboard.

Application

1. Before preparing a graph, decide specifically what it is that i
   to be portrayed.

2. Keep graphs simple but accurate.

3. Utilize different colors and textures for more eye-catchin
   representation.

4. Make the total chart *self*-explanatory. All information shoul
   be on the graph so that it can be understood without narratio

5. Label graphs with titles.

6. If symbols are used, make sure they are clearly defined.

HANDOUTS

Description

Materials to aid in communication---such as outlines, case studies, problems, data, and summaries---are given to each student, usually for personal retention.

Advantages or Special Purposes

1. Each student has an easy-to-see, permanent copy of the material.

2. The material is given to the student in some organized manner.

3. Information presented in this manner can stimulate thought or provide the basis for students to review at their leisure.

4. Information contained in handouts can readily serve as the basis for group discussion.

5. Having materials in the hands enhances visual sense appeal.

6. The learner with a visual impairment is less handicapped.

7. Handouts can be re-usable.

8. Handouts can be used with any size group.

9. It is possible to design handouts to require active learner participation.

Disadvantages or Limitations

1. It takes class time for students to read the material.

2. Confusion and disorder can occur while the handouts are being distributed.

3. Students may be reading the handouts when they should be doing something else.

4. If a handout is to be used over a number of days, some students may forget or lose theirs.

5. Spelling errors or "typos" may not create a very positive student feeling toward the teacher's language arts abilities.

6. Competent typing skills and duplicating equipment may not be readily available to the teacher.

7. It is difficult to use color.

Application

1. Plan handouts in advance so that they are properly tied-in with the subject.

2. Be sure your handouts are neat and accurate.

3. Be certain you have enough copies, and a few extras for replacing "lost" copies.

4. Tell the students what use they are to make of the handouts when they are received.

5. Pass out the printed material only when you are ready for the learners to begin reading immediately.

6. Avoid talking while distributing the handouts.

7. Distribute handouts in a predetermined and systematic fashion.

MOCK-UPS

Description

A Mock-up is an unscaled replica designed to simplify and clarify the workings of the object. The mock-up, which may be larger or smaller than the real thing, is generally constructed to show the "essential" parts and their functional relationship. A popular mock-up is the large replica flower with detachable parts that is to be found in many classrooms.

Advantages or Special Purposes

Mock-ups have all of the advantages of *realia* (see page 266) plus the following:

1. Mock-ups permit the observation of essential functions of the object.

2. Mock-ups can be made by the teacher and/or students, as well as purchased commercially.

3. By eliminating unnecessary details, the mock-up enables the learner to zero in on the material to be learned.

4. Mock-ups can be made larger or smaller than the real thing.

5. Mock-ups are generally working types which stress the actual operations involved in the functioning of the real object.

6. Having students build mock-ups enhances learning.

Disadvantages or Limitations

In general, mock-ups have the same limitations as *realia* plus the following disadvantages:

1. Mock-ups can be costly when purchased.

2. Making mock-ups can be time consuming for the teacher or th class.

3. Because mock-ups are not to scale, and because the parts ma be in a functional arrangement rather than actual order, student may not recognize the real object when faced with it.

4. Students need guidance in the construction of mock-ups.

Application

Using mock-ups includes all of the guidelines for the use of *model* (see page 257) plus the following:

1. Be sure the mock-up truly illustrates the functional factors o the real thing.

2. Have the students make mock-ups according to a planne sequence.

3. Be certain to give the students a picture of the scale an location of parts on the real thing.

4. Use mock-ups when it is essential for students to "see" how th real thing works.

MODELS OF REALIA

Description

Often the real thing cannot be used in the classroom. If this is due to size---either too large or too small an object---a scaled replica called a model can be used. Models are near-perfect replicas of the real thing. They are either reduced in scale or enlarged in scale. Examples of models are: train sets; model cars and planes; doll houses and furniture; and animal or human figurines.

Advantages or Special Purposes

Models have all of the advantages of *realia* (see page 266) plus the following:

1. Models enable the teacher to use items even when the real item is impractical due to size.

2. Models can be purchased from commercial firms or they can be homemade by the teacher and/or the students.

3. Having students make models enhances learning and provides motivation.

4. When students make models, many subject areas are combined in an inter-disciplinary manner.

5. Models come in working or non-working modes.

Disadvantages or Limitations

Models have the same deficiencies as the use of *realia* plus the following:

1. Buying models, especially working models, can be costly.

2. Producing home-made models can be costly as well as very time consuming.

3. Since models are built to scale, students may misinterpret the actual size of the object.

Application

Using models, follow the same guidelines as when using *realia*, plus the following:

1. Present the model in such a manner as to help the learner understand the size of the real object.

2. Be sure the model is in definite proportion to the real object, of the same color, etc.

3. Use working models when movement is essential to understanding the lesson.

OPAQUE PROJECTOR

Description

The opaque project is used to project photographs, drawings, book pages and the like onto a screen for group viewing. It performs this function by lamp illumination of the material with the image being reflected by a mirror through a lens onto a screen.

Advantages or Special Purposes

1. Materials such as pictures which lose much in reproduction processes can be viewed naturally.

2. Color can be projected.

3. Small objects are magnified so they can be viewed by a group.

4. "Valuable" prints, pictures, etc. can be viewed with minimum damage due to handling by numerous people.

5. Tracings and enlargements of printed or pictured materials can be made by projecting onto a blank sheet of paper.

Disadvantages or Limitations

1. Opaque projectors are relatively heavy and bulky.

2. The room usually needs to be very dark.

3. Heat from the projector can damage the materials being projected.

4. Opaque projectors are expensive.

Application

1. Since opaque projectors are usually scarce, be sure to reserve one for the day you plan to use it.

2. Besides scarcity, the opaque projector may be in need of repair; thus the teacher should always have a Plan B just in case.

3. Practice with the projector in advance of the lesson so that the machine is properly placed to ensure maximum viewing effectiveness.

4. Pictures must be flat or parts of the image will be out of focus.

5. As with all sub-strategies, the material must fit the presentation.

6. If you can't find one in your building, look for it in an out-of-the-way closet, basement, attic, etc.

OVERHEAD TRANSPARENCIES

Description

The overhead projector, by means of light passage through a transparency, enables the instructor to project pictures and drawings large enough for use with a group.

Advantages or Special Purposes

1. The teacher can maintain eye contact while using the overhead.

2. Transparencies can be made professionally or by the teacher.

3. Color can be used.

4. Transparencies may be written on and then the writing can be removed afterwards.

5. Transparencies are easy to prepare.

6. Overlays can be used for sequenced presentations.

7. Transparencies are reusable.

8. They can be used with both large and small groups.

9. Transparencies can be used with normal room lighting.

10. Overhead projectors are simple to operate.

11. Transparencies can be made with copy machines (be sure to use the correct film type with the correct temperature setting.)

Disadvantages or Limitations

1. The overhead projector, while educationally a bargain, costs money, especially if each classroom is to have one.

2. As with any mechanical device, moving the projector around can result in damage.

3. Occasionally, transparencies become overheated, causing them to be damaged.

4. Professionally prepared transparencies cannot be easily modified as information changes.

5. The process of getting the projection image at a height where all can see often produces a "keystoning" effect.

Application

1. Make sure the overhead projector is available when you need it.

2. Have your transparencies prepared and organized in advance of their use.

3. Turn the projector off when changing transparencies so as not to distract the viewers.

4. Use a pencil or small pointer to point out important information directly on the transparency.

5. A cellophane roll or blank sheets of acetate can be used in the same way as the chalkboard.

6. Students should be encouraged to learn to use the overhead in making student presentations.

PICTURES

Description

The term "pictures" refers to flat, opaque, still pictures which may be photographs or pictures from magazines, books, or newspapers.

Teachers often use pictures in one of two ways. One is to teach children to "read" pictures. The other is to transmit information through pictures. It is the contention of the authors that both the uses are always involved.

Advantages or Special Purposes

1. Excellent pictures are available in limitless quantity and endless variety.

2. Pictures are very economical, often free.

3. Abstract ideas can be made real.

4. Pictures are effective in creating interest.

5. A tremendous amount of information can be contained in a well-chosen picture.

6. Pictures are more effective than oral or written statements alone.

7. Pictures can be used to trigger creative activities.

8. Pictures can be used as an evaluation technique.

9. Pictures can be used over and over again.

10. Still pictures can be used to reinforce previous impressions, to present new concepts or facts, or to form a basis from which to develop new meanings of abstractions.

11. Still pictures permit close-up detailed study at one's leisure.

Disadvantages or Limitations

1. Small pictures are difficult for a class to see.

2. Often pictures fail to present a scale of size or perspective. An 8" X 10" picture of an aircraft carrier gives no hint as to its size. A similar picture of a row boat could lead the learner to conclude that the row boat is larger than an aircraft carrier.

3. Too many pictures used at one time distract and confuse the learner.

4. It is easy for the teacher to be attracted by a beautiful picture which teaches little about the subject.

5. Unless proper care is taken, pictures can get torn, disordered, or lost.

6. Too much handling of pictures causes damage.

7. An organized, usable filing system takes time to develop and space to store.

Application

1. Pictures should be selected only in terms of their contribution to achieving the objectives of instruction.

2. Pictures should be easily seen, accurate, attractive, well-produced, and contain the information being taught.

3. Carefully select the proper number of pictures to be studied.

4. Mount pictures on hard paper and cover with lamination or a acrylic spray for protection.

5. Organize and file pictures according to a system which has meaning for you.

6. Get the pictures as close to the students as possible. Use an opaque projector if necessary for all to see.

REALIA

Description

Realia---real things---represent the actual conditions with which the learner will live. As such, realia should be used whenever possible. Real things are available. The task is to locate them and put them to use in helping students learn. Examples of realia are: insects; coins; rocks; plants; pets; and stamps.

Advantages or Special Purposes

1. Experience with real things with which one will interact in life is the best learning situation possible.

2. Real objects are plentiful and available everywhere.

3. Real items can be observed and handled, providing concrete learning experiences for the student.

4. Dealing with realia motivates the learner.

5. Realia can be used as part of the evaluation system.

6. Realia learning can be extended through the use of classroom or schoolwide displays.

Disadvantages or Limitations

1. Real things are not always readily available.

2. Realia are not always practical for use in the classroom:

   a. Size---a real object may be too large (a submarine) or too small (a single human cell) for classroom study.

     b.   Potential hazards---realia such as live animals, certain electrical and mechanical equipment, etc., can represent potential hazards for the learner and the teacher.

     c.   Cost---real objects often are expensive.

     d.   Need to maintain original structure---while some realia can be dismantled, many others cannot be, e.g., cutting open a person to see how the heart functions.

3.   Affective learning is unpredictable through realia.

4.   If left sitting around the classroom, realia can be a distraction.

5.   Storage and retrieval can create problems.

Application

1.   Be certain the real object enhances your objectives.

2.   Make whatever advanced arrangements are necessary for proper use of the realia.

3.   Costs can often be minimized by borrowing real items from members of the community.

4.   Keep the realia under wraps until you are ready to use them; after using, remove the potential distractor from sight.

5.   Students should be encouraged to help in locating and acquiring realia for classroom use.

6.   Develop a system of storage and retrieval which will be functional.

SIMULATION DEVICES

Description

Simulation devices are designed to give the student a set of experiences under near real-to-life conditions. Simulations, long used in military and business, are gaining more use in schools now. Some of the devices used include: driver trainers, telephone kits, and mannequins for artificial respiration and cardiopulmonary resuscitation (CPR). The future will provide us with the ability to use vitual reality as a teaching tool. Our students pioneered the concept with their TV's, Nintendo and Sega games. At present this technology is too costly for general educational use, but more affordable versions are on the horizon.

Advantages or Special Purposes

Simulation devices have the same strengths as *realia* (see page 266) plus the following:

1. Learning experiences can be held in the classroom or simulator laboratory rather than away from the school.

2. Students can practice in complete safety to themselves, others and the equipment.

3. Feedback is presented to the teacher and learner through behavior-recording instruments.

4. Learning by doing is usually faster and provides better retention than "book-learning."

5. Simulation provides the opportunity to function under "normal" and "abnormal" conditions.

Disadvantages or Limitations

Simulation devices share the same weaknesses as *realia* (see page 266) plus the following:

1. Simulation devices are usually extremely expensive.

2. Since simulation devices often are electronic in nature, school systems may not be able to provide maintenance services locally.

3. Some simulation devices are rather sensitive and break down under student use or abuse.

4. Simulation may provide a sense of "false" security for the student as mistakes in simulation do not lead to the same type of consequences as in real life.

Application

Simulation devices should be used in the same manner as *realia*, plus the following:

1. Be sure students realize the limitations of simulation in regard to real-life consequences.

2. Stress the use of feedback devices for students as a means to improve performance.

3. Encourage students to use and maintain the condition of these devices properly.

4. Become aware of normal maintenance practices and procedures and apply them as required.

5. Use Simulation devices to *enhance* instruction and not as a means to do all of the instruction.

SLIDES

Description

Slides are individual pictures which are projected on a screen for a class to view. Slides can be used with or without sound. The use of slides with sound is covered in the *slide-tape* sub-strategy.

Advantages or Special Purposes

1. Slides add realism to class presentations.

2. Slides can be home-made to fit the teacher's needs or purchased from a commercial outfit.

3. Slides are small, thus storage is not a problem.

4. Slide projectors are usually available to teachers.

5. Slide projectors are portable and relatively inexpensive.

6. All kinds of pictures, drawings, charts and diagrams can be put on slides.

7. Remote control of the slide projector is often available, permitting the teacher to move about the room.

8. Automatic focus is often available on slide projectors.

9. Slides are flexible in that various sequential arrangements can be made to fit the situation.

10. Slides can be readily updated by simple replacement.

Disadvantages or Limitations

1. Since slides usually are not captioned, the teacher must help students understand the material being viewed.

2. Because they are small, individual slides can be easily lost or become disarranged.

3. A great deal of preparation and rehearsal time is required.

4. The room generally needs to be darkened, thus causing the teacher to lose eye contact with the students.

5. Too many slides or a too rapid succession of slides can be distracting.

6. Focused discussion is often difficult in a darkened room.

7. Teachers may lack the skill or knowledge to make slides.

8. Commercially produced slides may not treat the subject matter in the manner desired by the teacher.

9. Students cannot easily take notes in a darkened room.

Application

1. Prepare by defining purposes and organizing and numbering slides to fit your objectives.

2. Rehearse your presentation to ensure the best utilization of time, understanding of the material, proper lighting, and functioning of the machine.

3. If you need to rely on notes in a darkened room, use a small flashlight, directed so as not to reflect in the students' eyes.

4. Speak about an image only while it is on the screen.

5. Use proper spacing of slides, approximately 3-5 slides per minute.

6. Use a pointer to indicate details you want the viewers to observe more closely.

7. Since the slide projector can get hot, keep the projector off and the room lights on at the beginning while introducing the lesson and at the end while conducting the summary.

8. Any lists or other information which students should have noted should be reviewed or presented on a handout.

SLIDE-TAPES

Description

The slide-tape sub-strategy involves the projection of individual pictures on a screen with an accompanying commentary via audio tape. Although disc records are sometimes used, audio-tape cassettes predominate.

The characteristics of the slide sub-strategy and the audio-tape sub-strategy are combined in using slide-tapes. Therefore, only the unique features of the slide-tape combination will be considered.

Advantages or Special Purposes

1. Voice and/or music can be used to enhance the visual presentation.

2. Slide-tapes can be either of the home-made variety or commercially produced.

3. Slides can be advanced by a "beep" signal from the audio tape, or they can be advanced manually by the teacher.

4. Slides and audio cassettes require little storage space.

Disadvantages or Limitations

1. The learner's attention can quickly wander from a taped voice.

2. Slide-tapes are less flexible since it requires modification of both the slides and the tape to make changes in the presentation.

3. The more structured approach of the slide-tape limits spontaneous discussion by class members.

4. Because two pieces of equipment are used, there is twice the likelihood of equipment malfunction.

5. Using a manual slide advance with tape requires the teacher to "know" the lesson or to follow a script---which is difficult in a darkened room.

6. Automatic triggering of slides by a signal from the audio tape sometimes malfunctions, causing visuals and sound to get "out of sync."

7. Students cannot easily take notes in a darkened room.

Application

1. Plan in advance by knowing your objectives and rehearsing your presentation.

2. Use live, personal narration rather than audio-tape if at all possible.

3. Be sure *both* the visual and auditory images fit your objectives.

4. Provide for a meaningful introduction and for a discussion time at the end since use of slide-tapes precludes spontaneous discussion during the presentation.

5. Any significant specific data which you expect students to retain should be either reviewed or presented on a handout.

TELEPHONE SYSTEMS

Description

Telephone systems may be used to tap into live and recorded resources. An individual or any number of individuals, who have expertise or information of interest to students, may be interconnected to a classroom, meeting room, or a room as large as an auditorium, as well as a multi-site hookup. Interactive Video, Audiographics, and Networked Instruction are the three primary programs that generate what is called "Distance Learning." These systems give students the opportunity to hear and see pertinent information and ideas and also share their feedback with the speakers, instructors, and other participants. The systems may accommodate local and long distance input. A "homework hotline" may be established to facilitate assignment and information sharing with absentees and also act as a deterrent to truancy. This sub-strategy will grow significantly as current technology becomes more affordable.

Advantages or Special Purposes

1. Students are involved in "live" active communication.

2. Students have access to up-to-date information and ideas.

3. Active listening skills are reinforced.

4. Critical thinking skills are enhanced.

5. Speakers save time by not traveling.

6. Resources are maximized.

7. More students are served in more locations with fewer teachers.

8. Promotes collaborative and hands-on learning.

9. May also be used for teacher and parental education.

Disadvantages or Limitations

1. Initial costs and maintenance costs may be prohibitive for a single school or district.

2. Electronic malfunctions are not rare.

3. Extraordinary planning is required.

4. Advanced technology frightens some users.

Application

1. Contact all participants; explain the procedures and confirm dates for the Distance Learning program.

2. Contact the telephone company and make arrangements for date or dates of the Distance Learning program. (Remember time zone differences!)

3. Prepare students for the nature of the program as well as processes to be used.

4. Develop active listening skills and critical thinking skills prior to the program.

5. Encourage active feedback participation.

6. Follow-up the session with small group and large group discussions, questions, and suggestions.

7. Have students develop ideas for new programs.

VIDEO TAPES/FILMS

Description

Films come in the forms of film (8mm and 16m), video tape, and 8mm loops and cartridges. They are rentable and/or easily purchased.

Advantages or Special Purposes

1. "Movies" are inherently high in motivation.

2. They are useful in showing movement or relationships.

3. They are adaptable for individuals, small and large groups.

4. They ensure a consistency in material presented.

5. They require very little reading skill on the part of the student to absorb the contained message.

6. Films/Videos are available on almost any topic desired.

7. Student production of films or video tapes is an excellent project method.

8. VCR's are relatively inexpensive.

9. VCR tapes can be edited/indexed to show only the critical highlights.

Disadvantages or Limitations

1. Locating films with exact content desired can be a problem, and getting them on the date needed is usually chancey.

2. Previewing films for free on a rental basis is nearly impossible.

3. Film projection equipment is expensive to purchase and maintain.

4. Mechanical and operational problems are not infrequent with projection equipment.

5. Some films may run the length of an entire class period, leaving little time for discussion or processing.

Application

1. In purchasing, renting or borrowing films, order far enough in advance to allow time for confirmation. This prevents being caught short on the day you plan to show them.

2. Become thoroughly acquainted with film or tape content. Make notes of important terms, concepts and facts, plus discussion and assessment questions.

3. Set up film or video tape *prior* to class.

4. Before showing, discuss with the class the objectives of the film or tape, important terms, and questions to be answered by the use of this sub-strategy.

5. Show the film with proper attention to viewer comfort: seating, temperature, ventilation, and lighting.

6. After the showing, lead discussion on previously established terms, concepts, facts and questions.

7. Tie in with content currently being studied.

Part Three

ASSESSMENT OF LEARNING

ASSESSMENT OF LEARNING

Good assessment demands that you know and are able to articulate your major instructional outcomes. Outcomes determine your performance criteria so that you can evaluate your degree of success. What do you want your students to accomplish in a unit, in a course, in a discipline, or across disciplines? What should students be able to do at the completion of a unit, a course of study, or a year of study that they were not able to do before? What critical areas of student development do you want to influence? Stephen Covey says it best in his book *The 7 Habits of Highly Effective People,* "Begin with the end in mind." What is it that you want your students to know, to be able to do, and to feel or believe after the learning has occurred?

The answers to these questions define your teaching priorities and represent the primary target for your instructional activities. It also establishes the assessment tasks that students will have to perform. Students will have the opportunity to acquire the knowledge and skills that you are teaching and an opportunity to demonstrate their level of proficiency in those you deem most important.

LEARNER OUTCOME PRINCIPLES

Clarity of Focus
> The instruction, activities and interactions should be designed around the clearly defined outcomes we want all students to learn.

Ample Opportunity
> You must deliberately provide all students with the time and instructional support they need to reach the intended outcomes.

High Expectations
> You must consistently expect all students to meet reasonably high performance standards.

Begin at the End

Student learning experiences are designed to directly reflect and facilitate the outcomes that students are ultimately expected to demonstrate successfully.

Learner outcomes usually start with larger more global statements such as these outcomes from the Carnegie Council's Report on Adolescent Development: *What do we want every young adolescent to know, to feel, to be able to do upon emerging from that educational and school related experience? Our answer is embodied in five characteristics associated with being an effective human being.* Our 15-year-old will be:
1. An intellectually reflective person;
2. A person enroute to a lifetime of meaningful work;
3. A good citizen;
4. A caring and ethical individual; and,
5. A healthy person

As outcomes work their way through the disciplines they become more specific, but still broad. For example, students will be able to demonstrate the following cognitive skills:
1. Communicate effectively in writing---to write good descriptions, to write persuasively, and to write stories.
2. Communicate effectively orally.
3. Analyze literature using plot, character, setting, and theme.
4. Analyze issues using primary source and reference material.
5. Use Algebra to solve everyday problems.
6. Analyze current events from historical, political, geographic, and multicultural perspectives.
7. Design and conduct studies to aid decision-making about current and every day problems.
8. Use the scientific method.
9. Use different media to express what they know.

As the outcomes work their way through a specific discipline, such as science, they may look like this:
Students will be able to:
1. Develop a hypothesis.

2. Design experiments.
3. Draw inferences from data.
4. Use observation and analyze similarities and differences in phenomena.
5. Work with laboratory equipment.

A teacher's unit plan in a science curriculum might have these outcomes for a three lesson unit that introduces them to the science lab. Students will be able to:
1. Safely use all lab equipment.
2. Accurately gather and measure data in metric units.
3. Record data in a meaningful graph format.
4. Present conclusions of the experiment in written format.
5. Work collaboratively with a lab partner.

Outcomes get more specific by unit level and continue to become more focused as they are applied to direct student interaction.
Students will be able to demonstrate ability to accurately use metric measures:
1. Celsius - temperature
2. Milliliter - volume
3. Millimeter - length

These outcomes are very specific, easy to measure and document, and, therefore, assure student learning.

As we begin the process of assessing student progress and development we should familiarize ourselves with some of the more traditional ways of student assessment.

TEACHER-MADE TESTS

On the topic of testing most teacher education textbooks stress the use of tests to measure instructional effectiveness. However, most teachers use tests to furnish a basis for assigning a grade. Rather than become embroiled in a philosophical discussion---since teachers would still use tests for assigning grades and test experts would still stress tests as a measure of instructional effectiveness---let us say that tests can be used for both purposes. Also, they can be misused for either purpose.

Whatever the case, the several types of testing avenues available to the classroom teacher have inherent qualities much like the instructional strategies in this book. Our aim here is to help teachers better use the testing avenues available to them. This approach does not preclude the need for teachers to become aware of statistics as applied to testing. In fact, all teachers should have formal study in the proper application of statistics to the classroom situation, and not limited only to testing. Our focus is upon usage of oral and written means of classroom testing as designed by the teacher. Each of these means will be examined in terms of its (1) *definition and description,* (2) *advantages or special purposes,* (3) *disadvantages or limitations,* and (4) *guidelines for maximum utilization.*

Before proceeding directly to this examination, certain testing concepts must be considered. These concepts will be used as criteria by which testing options will be compared.

The first concept is that of *validity.* In test jargon, validity is often said to be the degree to which a test measures what it purports to measure. For our use in examining testing approaches, we are interested in what types of behaviors the various approaches best measure. Validity is the most important of the concepts since we must be sure we are measuring what we think we are measuring.

Next comes *reliability.* Reliability deals with the consistency of results in measuring the same thing. One way of looking at reliability is to expect each of a group of students to get the same, or nearly the same, scores on a test-retest basis.

The third criterion we will deal with is *objectivity*. Objectivity really deals with the scoring of the test. If, in the scoring process, the scorer's subjective judgment does not enter in, the test is objective. In this case, the student would get the same score no matter who scored the test.

The fourth factor is *comprehensiveness*. Comprehensiveness refers to the degree of sampling of what has been taught. Obviously on a semester exam, a teacher cannot test everything taught during the entire semester. However, a proportionate sampling of the major teachings can be made. The wider the range of subject matter tested and the truer the proportion tested, the more *comprehensive* the test is said to be.

The fifth area considered deals with *practical matters* involved in testing. These matters include (1) the time involved in constructing and scoring the tests, (2) the efficient use of class time for testing, and (3) the ease of constructing, administering, and scoring the test.

As the various testing approaches are examined, there will sometimes be a focus on test "type" and other times a focus on test "item." The reasons for this will be seen as each approach is examined.

COMPLETION

Definition and Description

Completion, or fill-in-the-blank, items are those in which the student provides one or more missing words. This type of question calls for the students to recall the proper response.

Advantages or Special Purposes

1. Completion items are best used in cases where the student is expected to recall specific facts (names, dates, places, events, definitions, etc.).

2. Little opportunity for guessing is provided.

3. Completion items are relatively easy to construct.

4. This item is more comprehensive than the *essay* type in that it provides for greater sampling of learning in the same amount of time.

Disadvantages or Limitations

1. Overuse of the completion test approach often creates an overemphasis on memorization on the part of the learner.

2. The higher level cognitive skills are not tested in this manner.

3. While less subjective than the *essay* item, the completion item still lacks some objectivity. The teacher often will need to decide if the given answer is "close enough" or "means the same thing."

4. It is tempting for the teacher to copy statements directly from the textbook, thus creating poor items.

5.   Teachers often use too many blanks, leaving a vague and ambiguous puzzle to be solved.

Guidelines for Maximum Utilization

1.   Use only one blank in an item.

2.   Write the item so specifically that there can be one and only one answer. (Or, plan to give credit for more than one.)

3.   Place the blank at the end of the statement. If this is difficult, write the item in question form.

4.   Paraphrase sentences taken from the textbook.

5.   Make a model with the correct answers for use in scoring.

Questions to Promote Discussion

Below are questions which contain some errors. Using the above material, identify the errors and explain how the items should have been constructed. (Cite the specific statement in the text whenever possible.)

Completion Items (Not necessarily parts of the same test)

1.   A. Lincoln was born in _____.
2.   Paraphrase sentences taken from the _____.
3.   _____ the blanks at the end of the statement.
4.   _____ only one _____ in _____ _____.

ESSAY

Definition and Description

In an essay examination, the student writes a response to one or more questions requiring an answer of at least a sentence. Such responses range from a simple sentence for an elementary school student to one requiring several days and many pages for a graduate student.

Essay examinations can be used to measure either content (the answer) or process (how well written) or both. A common problem is that teachers often have not decided or have not explained to the student what "counts." Thus the student is sure to ask immediately before answering the first question, "Does spelling count?"

Advantages or Special Purposes

1. Essay questions are best used for objectives dealing with the improvement of written skills, interpretation and use of data, creative expression, organization of ideas, and positional or thematic development.

2. Knowing that essay items will be used usually motivates the student to study more thoroughly.

3. While the construction of good essay questions is more difficult than is generally believed, they are easier to construct than most types of test items.

4. "Cheating" or copying another's work is virtually impossible with proper use of essay tests.

5. The opportunity for guessing is almost non-existent.

Disadvantages or Limitations

1. Essay items are the most subjective of all of the test items. Their lack of objectivity has been widely demonstrated and discussed in research.

2. With such a lack of objectivity, the essay item is low in reliability.

3. Comprehensiveness of the essay item is poor since a relatively little amount of material can be covered in a given time.

4. Large amounts of time are needed to score essay items.

5. Essay questions are inefficient in the use of class time since the physical act of writing is much slower than the answering of objective-type items.

6. Essay items are not easy to score. They require reading time, and students have a variety of ways of expressing themselves, which demands more time for interpretation.

Guidelines for Maximum Utilization

1. Use the essay means of evaluation only for those objectives for which it is best suited.

2. Decide whether you are concerned about content or process, or both, and explain this to students before testing.

3. State the question as specifically as possible so that students will know what you want.

4. Minimize the weakness of subjectivity by:
   a. Developing a model-outline answer against which all student answers can be compared;

      b.   Scale the number of points to be awarded for each portion of the model-outline answer;

      c.   Score all papers anonymously; and,

      d.   When several specific essay questions are used, score the first question on each paper before going on to the next question, and so on.

5.   Explain the reason why each incorrect answer is not considered correct.

6.   Review, in class, the model-outline answer for each item and how you scored the papers. Listen to arguments.

7.   Beside each test item, list how many points each is worth, thus allowing students a basis for gauging the relative importance of each question.

Questions to Promote Discussion

Below are questions which contain some errors. Using the above material, identify the errors and explain how the items should have been constructed. (Cite the specific statement in the text whenever possible.)

Essay Items (Not necessarily parts of a single test)

1.   Discuss the Civil War.

2.   List, in order, the first ten presidents of the U.S.

3.   Compare and contrast Communism and Socialism in terms of:
      a.   the control of industry.
      b.   the ownership of property.
      c.   efficiency of agricultural practices.

MATCHING

Definition and Description

The Matching item is a set of two lists in which each item in one list is related to an item in the other list. The instructions given explain the basis on which the various items are related. For ease of identification, one column (the left) is often called the "statement" and the other (the right) the "answer."

Advantages or Special Purposes

1. The Matching item is best used for those objectives which require the learner to associate related data.

2. Objectivity in scoring is present in this item.

3. This item is comprehensive in that large amounts of learning can be sampled in a short period of time.

4. Advantage #3 insures efficient use of class time.

5. Little time and effort is needed in scoring matching items.

Disadvantages or Limitations

1. Often, a sufficient quantity of related data does not exist to consider using matching items.

2. When an insufficient amount of related data exists teachers often manufacture items, thus creating poor questions.

3. Instructions regarding the basis of matching are often difficult to write.

4. Directions for marking the correct answers are difficult to write.

Guidelines for Maximum Utilization

1. Use matching items only where a sufficient number of related data exists.

2. Items should be homogeneous. This means that all "statements" and "answers" must be dealing with the same thing (people or places or dates, etc.).

3. Explain the basis for matching.

4. Avoid giving grammatical clues.

5. Avoid perfect matching so that students do not get the last answer by the "process of elimination," i.e., have extra items in the answer column.

6. Keep the lists under a dozen "statements" and "answers."

7. Arrange the "answers" in some order, generally alphabetical, to aid in finding the correct response.

8. Present clear directions regarding the manner in which the student is to indicate his/her response.

9. Electronic scanning devices are relatively inexpensive and significantly reduce the time to correct teacher tests using the *matching, multiple choice,* and *true-false* items. It also provides an itemized printout of student responses for each question.

Questions to Promote Discussion

Below are questions which contain some errors. Using the above material identify the errors and explain how the items should have been constructed. (Cite the specific statement in the text whenever possible.)

Matching

Match the following:

(Statement)   (Answer)

1. Discovered the Law of Gravity   a. Mississippi

2. First president of the U.S.   b. 1976

3. Longest river in the U.S.   c. Newton

4. Largest city in Illinois   d. Harvard

5. First college in the U.S.   e. Chicago

6. Bicentennial.   f. Washington

MULTIPLE-CHOICE

Definition and Description

With the multiple-choice item, the learner selects from among two or more alternatives the one which correctly completes the statement or answers the question. The incomplete statement or question presented is called the stem.

This item type seems to be held in higher esteem by tests and measurements people than by classroom teachers. Technically, the multiple-choice item is a superior item. However, it must be recognized that the item has some weaknesses which bother classroom teachers.

Advantages or Special Purposes

1. The multiple-choice item can be used to measure a wide variety of objectives.

2. Scoring can be done on an objective basis.

3. Reliability is generally good.

4. These items permit a fairly wide sampling of learning in a short period of time; thus they are high in comprehensiveness and efficient in use of class time.

5. Multiple-choice items are easily and quickly scored.

Disadvantages or Limitations

1. Multiple-choice items are the most difficult to construct.

2. In constructing these items, much time is required.

3. Because test "experts" extol the virtues of multiple-choice items, teachers often "force" material or objectives into the multiple-choice format when they should be measeued in other ways.

4. Multiple-choice items are not entirely free from the "guessability" factors---e.g., one item is usually easily eliminated and gives a student a 1 in 3 chance of guessing the correct item.

Guidelines for Maximum Utilization

1. Use multiple-choice items to measure only those objectives for which they are compatible.

2. Use at least four alternatives for each statement or question.

3. Write in question form.

4. Insure that each alternative is plausible enough to be at least considered correct by the student.

5. Avoid grammatical "hints" in the stem as to the correct answer (singular-plural, etc.).

6. Avoid the use of the word "not" in the stem. If "not" must be used, underline the word so the student doesn't perceive it as a "trick" question.

7. Avoid any pattern of correct answer position. Some teachers tend to make the last alternative the correct one.

8. Make all alternatives of near-equal length.

9. If you use both "all of the above" and none of the above" in the same item, do so in that order.

10. Avoid using either "all of the above" and "none of the above" *only* when it is the correct answer. Use it at times when it is not the correct answer.

Questions to Promote Discussion

Below are questions which contain some errors. Using the above material, identify the errors and explain how the items should have been constructed. (Cite the specific statement in the text whenever possible.)

Multiple-Choice (Not necessarily items of a single test)

1. How many states are there in the United States?
   a. 50
   b. 48

2. A unit of weight is an
   a. mile
   b. foot
   c. ounce
   d. minute

3. The primary colors are
   a. red
   b. yellow
   c. blue
   d. none of the above
   e. all of the above

ORAL TESTING

Definition and Description

Oral examinations in which a group of established experts attempt to assess the knowledge of an individual neophyte are commonplace in the graduate schools of universities. Below that level, however, the use of oral examinations is usually limited to the teacher asking questions of individual students in the classroom setting.

Basically, an oral examination can be concerned with either content or process. By "content" is meant that the substance of the student's answer is of prime import rather than how well the answer was said. "Process," on the other hand, refers to the manner in which the student answered the question. In this case the concern is for the development of oral skills.

Advantages or Special Purposes

1. The oral approach can be used for those objectives which require the learner to explain, tell, name, etc.

2. This approach is the only one which can be used to assess the learner's development of oral skills.

3. An average amount of time is required to construct questions.

4. Some students are psyched out by written tests and perform with more validity on an oral examination.

Disadvantages or Limitations

1. The oral approach to testing lacks objectivity in scoring. This is why teams of judges are used in speech contests and debates. The subjectivity of the scorer enters into the scoring.

2. Since this means of testing lacks objectivity, it also lacks reliability.

3. Comprehensiveness is low since the teacher can ask only a limited number of questions in a given period of time, thus limiting the learning sampled.

4. Class time is not efficiently used since the other students are uninvolved while one student is participating.

5. Good questions are difficult to design. Too often teachers do this "off the top of their heads," the result being vague and unclear questions.

6. Students often give poor answers because they lack oral skills, not because they don't know the information.

7. Giving incorrect responses or not being able to respond in front of their peers often impairs students' self-esteem.

8. Teachers often are unsure of whether they are measuring content or process, or both.

9. Scoring is difficult unless all students have the same questions.

Guidelines for Maximum Utilization

1. Use oral testing basically to measure the development of oral skills.

2. If you must use oral testing for other purposes, do so sparingly and follow the remaining guidelines.

3. Decide whether you are measuring content or process. If you are not specifically measuring oral skill development, focus on content only.

4. Write out your questions in advance, being sure they are clear and unambiguous. (Refer to the *questioning* strategy for help on this.)

5. Make sure the questions proportionately sample the content taught.

6. Ask the question, pause, then call on a student. This will encourage all students to think about the answer.

7. Avoid a pattern of calling on people, alphabetically, down the row, etc. A pattern known by the students means one only has to think when his/her turn comes.

8. Do not make judgments on only one or a few samplings. You may have asked a good student the only question he/she can't answer.

9. Realize that any feedback you have received is limited since all students do not answer all questions.

Questions to Promote Discussion

1. What is the major use which can be made of oral testing? Why?

2. What is the chief weakness of oral testing? Why?

3. What would you do to compensate for the weakness mentioned in response to Question #2?

PERFORMANCE TESTING

Definition and Description

In performance testing, the student is required to perform some physical feat or demonstrate some skill which has been taught. Usually this type of testing is applied to kinesthetic learning. Generally students are tested individually, although it is possible to measure objectives aimed at team or group skill development.

Advantages or Special Purposes

1. Performance testing is best used to measure learning objectives concerned with skill development.

2. Learning is directly measured by having students doing rather than writing or talking about doing.

3. As students realize their need to demonstrate what is to be learned, motivation to learn is often increased.

4. Models of performance to be reached often improve the learner's performance.

5. Knowing the performance standard to be reached lets the learner work individually with efficiency to reach the standard.

Disadvantages or Limitations

1. Performance testing is subjective in scoring. (This is why competitive performances are often scored by several judges, with the high and low scores thrown out.)

2. Lacking objectivity, performance testing is thus low in reliability.

3. Performance testing is low in comprehensiveness. Students are generally tested one at a time, thus, only a few skills can be measured.

4. It is often necessary to put in a great amount of time to set up a performance test, especially if an apparatus is used.

5. Scoring takes time, especially to translate the performance effectively into a set of meaningful symbols for the learner's benefit.

6. Class time is not efficiently used since the rest of the students are not meaningfully involved while the one student is performing.

7. Discipline problems often arise among those "sideline" students not involved in the performance evaluation being conducted.

Guidelines for Maximum Utilization

1. Use performance testing only for learning for which it is valid, i.e., skill learning.

2. Demonstrate (or have demonstrated) and explain the standards of acceptable performance.

3. Explain the scoring system to be used and how each factor involved in the performance will be scored.

4. Keep the scoring system as simple as possible and based solely upon observable criteria.

5. Increase the objectivity of the scoring process by training student "verifiers" as scorers.

6. At the time of testing, have all required apparatus pre-arranged and checked out for operability and safety.

7. Define clearly what meaningful activity those students not directly involved in testing should be doing.

8. After the performance, explain to the student the significant strengths and weaknesses of his/her performance.

Questions to Promote Discussion

1. What do you consider to be the best use of performance testing? Why?

2. What do you consider to be the major drawback to performance testing? Why?

3. What would you do to minimize the effects of the drawback you listed in response to Question #2? Why?

TRUE-FALSE

Definition and Description

The student is presented with a statement which he or she must decide is either true or false. Teachers may use variations of the item in which students must provide the correct answer if the statement is false (true-false corrected).

Advantages or Special Purposes

1. True-false items are best used for those situations where the student is expected to identify the correct alternative from among two possibilities.

2. Scoring this item is highly objective.

3. A great amount of learning material can be sampled in a minimum amount of time, thus contributing to a high degree of comprehensiveness and efficient use of class time.

4. Items are relatively easy to construct, but not as easy as is often believed.

5. Not much time is required for scoring.

6. True-false tests can provide the teacher with a quick means to analyze the degree of general understanding a class has of a large block of material.

Disadvantages or Limitations

1. True-false items are susceptible to guessing. Students have a 50-50 chance of guessing correctly.

2. Because of this susceptibility to guessing, reliability is fairly low.

3. Students seem to be less motivated to study for this type of item, perhaps due to the "guessability" factor.

4. While true-false items are relatively easy to construct, they are often designed without the necessary planning, resulting in poorly worded items.

Guidelines for Maximum Utilization

1. Use true-false items only for those situations where two alternatives exist.

2. Use statements that are completely true or completely false. No "trick" questions.

3. Use short, simple sentences.

4. Paraphrase rather than copying directly from textbooks.

5. Avoid arranging an answer pattern which makes it easier to score, but can also be detected by students.

6. Avoid the hints given by statements using "always," "never," etc.

7. Aim for approximately one-half true answers and one-half false answers for a test.

8. Use "true-false corrected" and other variations to minimize the effects of guessing.

9. If the statement of an opinion is part of the question, state who is being cited.

Questions to Promote Discussion

Below are questions which contain some errors. Using the above material, identify the errors and explain how the items should have been constructed. (Cite the specific statement in the text whenever possible.)

True-False (Not necessarily parts of a single test)

_____	1.	Never punt on third down in football.
_____	2.	The big Ten is the toughest football conference.
_____	3.	Davy Crockett, who died at the Alamo, was once governor of Rhode Island.
_____	4.	In true-false questions, use short, simple sentences.

ALTERNATIVE METHODS OF ASSESSING

New teaching strategies and the emergence of integrated and cross-disciplinary skills has brought about the demand for new attention to systematic assessment. We now need ways to move from our sole emphasis on the products of student learning to a concern for the learning process. Learning is no longer thought to be a one-way transmission of knowledge from teacher to student. Skilled teachers use a variety of instructional strategies, from direct instruction to coaching, hands-on projects, discussion, and group processes to achieve their learning goals. Good teachers constantly assess how their students are doing, gather evidence of problems and progress, and adjust their instructional plans accordingly.

PRINCIPLES OF ASSESSMENT

1. Assessment is part of instruction.
2. Assessment methods and instruments are varied.
3. Assessment focuses on a broad range of abilities.
4. Assessment occurs continuously.
5. Ability is assessed in a variety of contexts.
6. Measures must be appropriate to the learners' development and cultural background.

ALTERNATIVE MODES OF ASSESSMENT
1. Open-ended experiences (e.g. mock trials, debates, simulations, etc.)
2. Logs and journals
3. Interviews
4. Writing samples
5. Video tapes
6. Culminating exhibitions (e.g. science fair, cultural fair, etc.)
7. Group tasks (e.g. cooperative learning end products)
8. Direct observation of student behavior (e.g. cooperation, leadership, ability to work independently)

9. Hands on experience (e.g. experiments, construction projects, task accomplishments)
10. Long term projects (e.g. unit activities, term papers, etc.)

PORTFOLIOS

When educators talk about authentic or alternative assessment the first strategy that comes to mind is usually portfolios. Portfolios provide two purposes for educators:
1. They are the receptacle for the collection of work (writing samples, videos, projects, journal entries, etc.)
2. They provide the criteria by which to evaluate an individual student or program.

Well conceived portfolios include student work representing both work in progress and "showpiece" samples, student reflection about their work (strengths and weaknesses), and evaluation criteria. Work in the portfolio should include both teacher and student selected samples.

Evaluation Criteria of Portfolios

CAP Generalized Rubric
(With permission of California State Department of Education)

Demonstrated Competence

Exemplary Response...Rating = 6
Gives a complete response with a clear, coherent, unambiguous, and elegant explanation; includes a clear and simplified diagram; communicates effectively to the identified audience; shows understanding of the open-ended problem's mathematical ideas and processes; identifies all the important elements of the problem; may include examples and counterexamples; presents strong supporting arguments.

Competent Response...Rating = 5
Gives a fairly complete response with reasonably clear explanations; may include an appropriate diagram; communicates effectively to the

identified audience; shows understanding of the problem's mathematical ideas and processes; identifies the most important elements of the problems; presents solid supporting arguments.

Satisfactory Response

Minor Flaws But Satisfactory...Rating = 4
Completes the problem satisfactorily, but the explanation may be muddled; argumentation may be incomplete; diagram may be inappropriate or unclear; understands the underlying mathematical ideas; uses mathematical ideas effectively.

Serious Flaws But Nearly Satisfactory...Rating = 3
Begins the problem appropriately but may fail to complete or may omit significant parts of the problem; may fail to show full understanding of mathematical ideas and processes; may make major computational errors; may misuse or fail to use mathematical terms; response may reflect an inappropriate strategy for solving the problem.

Inadequate Response

Begins, But Fails to Complete Problem...Rating = 2
Explanation is not understandable; diagram may be unclear; shows no understanding of the problem situation; may make major computational errors.

Unable to Begin Effectively...Rating = 1
Words do not reflect the problem; drawings misrepresent the problem situation; copies parts of the problem but without attempting a solution; fails to indicate which information is appropriate to problem.

No Attempt...Rating = 0

Constructing Comprehensive Portfolios

1. The work should be representative of what the student can really do.
2. Samples are identified as to the amount of support the individual student received (e.g. individual, coached or group).
3. The work includes student's comments (reflections and self-evaluations).
4. There is an evaluation criteria that is clearly defined. (See rubric.)
5. The portfolio is open to constant review and evaluation.
6. The portfolio becomes a basis for assessment by teacher, student, and parent(s).

Summary of Assessment

Assessment is critical to systemic educational success. Nothing raises more controversy, more confusion, and more emotion, than the topic of evaluation. Without accurate assessment it is impossible to determine if resources (human time, energy, materials, choices, and money) have been utilized to their optimum potential. But in the final analysis the expert educator knows that educational assessment has but one primary purpose in the teacher-student relationship: To improve teaching towards the maximizing of learning.

BIBLIOGRAPHY

Almy, M., *Logical Thinking in Second Grade*. New York: Teachers College Press, 1970.

Anderson, L., C. Evertson, and J. Brophy, "An Experimental Study of Effective Teaching in First-grade Reading Groups," *Elementary School Journal*, 79, 1979, 192-233.

Anderson, L. W., C. Scott, and N. Hutlock, "The Effects of a Mastery Learning Program on Selected Cognitive, Affective, and Ecological variables in Grades 1 through 6." Paper presented at the annual meeting of the Americal Educational Association, San Francisco, 1976.

Arlin, M., "Time Variability in Mastery Learning," *American Educational Research Journal*, 21, 1984, 103-20. Arlin, M., and J. Webster, "Time costs of Mastery Learning," *Journal of Educational Psychology*, 75, 1983. 187-96.

Aschner, C., *Strategies and Tactics in Secondary School Teaching: A Book of Readings*. New York: McMillan, 1968.

Aspy, David N., and Flora Roebuck, "An Investigation of the Relationship Between Student Levels of Cognitive Functioning and the Teacher's Classroom Behavior," *Journal of Educational Research*, 65, 1973, 365-368.

Atkinson, J.W., *Achievement Motivation*. New York: John Wiley & Sons, Inc., 1966.

Ausubel, D.P., "The Use of Advance Organizers in the Learning and Retention of Meaningful Verbal Material," *Journal of Educational Psychology*, 51, 1960, 267-72.

Axelrod, S., *Behavior Modification for the Classroom Teacher*. New York: McGraw-Hill, 1977.

Bachor, Dan, and Carol Crealock, "Instructional Strategies for Students with Special Needs," *Canadian Journal of Education*, 14, 1989, 504-5.

Bandura, A., *Principles of Behavior Modification*. New York: Holt, Rinehart & Winston, 1969.

Bandura, A., and B. Perloff, "Relative Efficacy of Self-monitored and Externally Imposed Reinforcement Systems," *Journal of Personality and Social Psychology*, 7, 1967, 111-16.

Bangert, R.L., and J.A. Kulik, Individualized Systems of
    Instruction: A Meta-analysis of Findings in Secondary
    Schools." Paper presented at the annual meeting of the
    American Educational Research Association. New York,
    March, 1982.

Bany, M., and L.V. Johnson, *Classroom Group Behavior: Group
    Dynamics in Education*. New York: MacMillan, Inc., 1964.

Barron, R.R., "The Effects of Advance Organizers upon the Reception,
    Learning, and Retention of General Science Concepts," DHEW
    Project No. 1B-030 ERIC Document Reproduction Service,
    ED 061554, 1971.

Barton, Judy A., "Problem-solving Strategies in Learning
    Disabled and Normal Boys: Developmental and Instructional
    Effects, *Journal of Educational Psychology*, 80, 1988, 184-91.

Becker, Wesley C., "Teaching Reading and Language to the
    Disadvantaged - What We Have Learned from Field
    Research," *Harvard Educational Review*, 47, 1978, 518-543.

Becker, W., and D. Carnine, (1980). "Direct Instruction: An
    Effective Approach for Educational Intervention with the
    Disadvantaged and Low Performers," in *Advances in Child
    Clinical Psychology*, eds. B. Lahey and A. Kazkin. (pp. 429-
    473). New York: Plenum, 1980.

Becker, Wesley C., and Russel Gursten, "A Follow Up of Follow
    Through: The Later Effects of the Direct Instruction Model
    on Children in the Fifth and Sixth Grades," *American
    Educational Research Journal*, 19, 1, Spring, 1982, 75-92.

Bender, William N., and Ikechukwu C. Ukeje, Instructional
    Strategies in Mainstream Classrooms: Prediction on the Strategies
    Teachers Select (Bender Classroom Structure Questionnaire),"
    Remedial and Special Education, 10, 1989, 23-30.

Bereiter, C., "How to Keep Thinking Skills from Going the Way
    of All Frills," *Educational Leadership*, 42, 1 Septermber,1984.

Block, James. *Mastery Learning: Theory and Practice*. New
    York: Holt, Rinehart, and Winston, 1971.

Block, J.W., and L.W. Anderson, *Mastery Learning in
    Classrooms*. N.Y.: Macmillan, 1975.

Bloom, B.S., "Mastery Learning," in *Mastery Learning: Theory and Practice,* ed. J.H. Block. New York: Holt, Rinehart, & Winston, 1971.

Bloom, B.S., "Time and Learning," *American Psychologist,* 29, 1974, 682-688.

Bloom, B.S., et al. *Taxonomy of educational objectives. Handbook I: Cognitive Domain.* New York: David McKay Co., 1956.

Boocock, S., and E. O. Schild, *Simulation Games in Learning.* Beverly Hills, Calif.: Sage Publications, Inc., 1968.

Bosch, Karen A. and Rebecca S. Bowers, "'Count Me In, Too,': Math Instructional Strategies for the Discouraged Learner," *The Clearing House,* 66, 1992, 104-6.

Breuer, Klaus and Halyna Hajovy, "Adaptive Instructional Simulations to Improve Learning of Cognitive Strategies," *Educational Technology,* 27, 1987, 29-32.

Brown, J. W., Lewis, R.B., & Harcleroad, F.F., *AV Instruction: Technology, Media and Methods.* New York: McGraw-Hill Book Co., 1977.

Callahan, Sterling G., *Successful Teaching in Secondary Schools.* Glenview, IL: Scott, Foresman & Co., 1966.

Carroll, J.B., "A Model of School Learning," *Teachers College Record,* 64, 1963, 722-733.

Carroll, J.B., "A Revisionist Model of School Learning," *Review of Education,* 3, 1977, 155-167.

Chesler, M., and R. Fox, *Role-Playing Methods in the Classroom.* Chicago: Science Research Associates, Inc., 1966.

Chung, Jaesam, "Collaborative Learning Strategies: The Design of Instructional Environments for the Emerging New School," *Educational Technology,* 31, 1991, 15-22.

Cohen, E., *Designing Groupwork.* NY: Teachers College Press, 1986.

Collins, K., "The Importance of Strong Confrontation in an Inquiry Model of Teaching," *School Science and Math,* 69, (7), 1969, 615-617.

Colvin, Geoffrey, and George M. Sugai, "Proactive Strategies for
    Managing Social Behavior Problems: An Instructional Approach,"
    Education and Treatment of Children, 11, 1988,
    341-8.
Covey, Steven, *The 7 Habits of Highly Effective People*. NY: Simon &
    Schuster, 1992.
Dictionary of Education. Ed. by Ralph B. Winn. DEDE: Greenwood
    Press, 1972.
DeCaro, James J, "Instructional Strategies in the Teaching of
    Perceptual and Psychomotor Skills," *Yearbook (American Council
    on Industrial Arts Teacher Education*, 1985, 154-80, 1985.
Duchastel, Philippe C., "Instructional Strategies for Simulation-
    Based Learning," *Journal of Educational Technology Systems*, 19,
    1990-91, 265-76.
Edmonds, Ronald R., "Effective Schools Research of Ronald
    Edmonds," *Educational Leadership*, 40, Dec., 1982, 13-15.
Ellis, Edwin S., Donald D. Deshler, and B. Keith Lenz, "An
    Instructional Model for Teaching Learning Strategies," *Focus on
    Exceptional Children*, 23, 1991, 1-24.
Ennis, Catherine D., "Instructional Strategies to Facilitate the
    Learning of Field-dependent Children, "*Early Child Development
    and Care*, 67, 1991, 95-109.
Erikson, Erik. *Childhood and Society*. New York: Norton, 1950.
Estes, W.E., ed. Handbook of Learning and Cognitive
    Processes, Vol. IV *Attention and Memory*. Hillsdale, N.J.:
    Lawrence Erlbaum Associates, 1976.
Estes, W.K., ed. *Handbook of Learning and Cognitive Process,
    Vol. II: Conditioning and Behavior Theory*. Hillsdale, J.J.:
    Lawrence Erlbaum Associates, 1975.
Evertson, C., "Differences in Instructional Activities in Higher
    and Lower-Achieving English and Math Classes," *The
    Elementary School Journal*, 82 (4), 1982, 329-350.
Feeley, Theodore, "The Concept of Inquiry in the Social
    Studies." Doctoral Dissertation, Stanford University, 1972.
Fisher, C.W., D. C. Berliner, N.N. Filby, R. Marliave, L.S.
    Ghen, and M.M. Dishaw, "Teaching Behaviors, Academic
    Learning Time, and Student Achievement: An Overview," in

Time to learn, eds. C. Denham and A. Liberman. Washington, D.C.: National Institute of Education, 1980.

Flanders, N., *Analyzing Teaching Behavior*. Reading, Mass: Addison-Wesley, 1970.

Flavell, J.H., *The Developmental Psychology of Jean Piaget*. Princeton, N.J.: Van Nortrand Reinhold, 1963.

Falvey, Mary A., "Community-based Curriculum; Instructional Strategies for Students with Severe Handicaps," *Education and Training in Mental Retardation*, 26, 1991, 110-11.

Good, Thomas L. & Jere Brophy, "Analyzing Classroom Interaction: A More Powerful Alternative, "*Educational Technology*, 11,1971, 36-41.

Gordon, William J.J, "The Integration of Creative Persons," paper delivered to Sloan Fellows, MIT, November, 1952.

Gordon, William J.J., "Some Environmental Aspects of Creativity," paper delivered to the Department of Defense, Fort Belvior, Va., December 1955.

Gordon, William J.J., "Creativity as a Process," paper delivered at the First Arden House Conference on Creative Process, October 10-12, 1956.

Gordon, William J.J., "Operational Approach to Creativity," *Harvard Business Review*, Vol. 34, No. 6 (November-December, 1956), pp. 41-51.

Gordon, William, J.J., (with Jerome Bruner), "Motivating the Creative Process," paper delivered at the Second Arden House Conference on Creative Process, May 7-10, 1957.

Gordon, William J.J., *SYNECTICS*. New York: Harper & Row, 1961.

Gordon, William J.J., "The Metaphorical Way of Knowing," *Education of Vision*, Gyorgy Kepes, editor. New York: George Braziller, 1965.

Gordon, W. J.J., *The Metaphorical Way of Learning and Knowing*. Cambridge, Mass.: S.E.S. Press, 1970.

Gordon, William J.J., and Poze, T., *The Basic Course in Synectics*. Cambridge: Porpoise Books, 1971.

Hall, B.P., Taylor, B., Kalven, J. & Rosen, L., *Developing Human Values*. Fond du Lac, WI: International Values Institute of Marian College, 1990.

Hullfish, H.G., and P.G. Smith, *Reflective Thinking: The Method of Education*. New York: Dodd, Mead & Company, 1961.

"Individually Prescribed Instruction," Philadelphia: Research for Better Schools. Unpublished manuscript, 1966.

"Individually Prescribed Instruction: Mathematics Continuum." Pittsburgh: University of Pittsburgh, Learning Research and Development Center, 1968.

"Instructional Strategies for Technology Education," *Yearbook (Council on Technology Teacher Education*, 1988, 1988, 3-207.

Ivany, George, "The Assessment of Verbal Inquiry in Elementary School Science," *Science Education*, 54 (4), 1969, 287-293.

Johnson, D.W., R.T. Johnson, J. Johnson, and D. Anderson, "The Effects of Cooperative vs. Individualized Instruction on Student Prosocial Behavior, Attitudes Toward Learning, and Achievement," *Journal of Educational Psychology*, 68, 1976, 446-452.

Johnson D.W., R.T. Johnson, and L. Scott. "The Effects of Cooperative and Individualized Instruction on Student Attitudes and Achievement," *Journal of Social Psychology*, 104, 1978, 207-216.

Johnson, D.W., G. Maruyama, R.T. Johnson, D. Nelson, and L. Skon, "Effects of Cooperative Competitive, and Individualistic Goal Structures on Achievement," *Psychological Bulletin*, 89, 1981, 47-62.

Joyce, B.R. "The 'Models of Teaching' Community: What Have We Learned?" Texas Tech Journal of Education. 2(2), 1975, 95-106.

Joyce, B.R., and B. Showers, "The Coaching of Teaching." *Educational Leadership, 40* (1), 1982, 4-16.

Kagan, S., *Cooperative Learning*. San Juan Capistrano, CA: Resources for Teaching, 1992.

Kahn, S.B., and J. Weiss, "The Teaching of Affective Responses," in *The Second Handbook of Research on Teaching*, ed. R.M.W. Travers. Chicago: McNally & Company, 1973.

Kamii, C. and R. DeVries, "Piaget-Based Curricula for Early Childhood Education," in *The Preschool in Action*, (rev. ed.), ed. Ron Parker, Boston: Allyn & Bacon, Inc., 1974.

Kerman, Sam, et al., "Teacher Expectation and Student Achievement," *Phi Delta Kappan*, 1979. Kilpatrick, W.H., *The Project Method*. New York: Teachers College Press, 1919.

Klausmeier, H.J., and C.W. Harris, *Analysis of Concept Learning*. New York: Academic Press, Inc., 1966.

Kleitsch, R.G., *Directory of Educational Simulations, Learning Games, and Didactic Units*. St. Paul, Minn.: Instructional Simulations, 1969.

Knudson, Ruth E., "Effects of Instructional Strategies, Grade, and Sex on Students' Persuasive Writing," *The Journal of Experimental Education*, 59, 1991, 141-52.

Lawson, A.E. et al., "Proportional Reasoning and Linguistic Abilities Required for Hypothetico-deduct Reasoning," *Journal of Research in Science Teaching*, 21 (4), 1984, 377-384.

Leshin, Cynthia B., Joellyn Pollock, and Charles M. Reigeluth, "Instructional Design Strategies and Tactics," *Educational Technology Research and Development*, 41, 1993, 97-9.

Lindvall, C.M., and J.O. Bolvin, "The Project for Individually Prescribed Instruction," Oakleaf Project, Unpublished manuscript, University of Pittsburgh, Learning Research and Development Center, 1966.

Lotan, Rachel A., Patricia E. Swanson, and Gerald K. Letendre, "Strategies for Detracked Middle Schools: Curricular materials, Instructional Strategies, and Access to Learning," *Middle School Journal*, 24, 1992, 4-14.

Low, William C., Michael L. Carson, and Steve Zlotolow, "A Data Base of Instructional Strategies," *The Journal of Computers in Mathematics and Science Teaching*, 7, 1988, 30-32.

McKinney, C., A. Warren, Guy Larkins, Mary Jane Ford, and John C. Davis, III, "The Effectiveness of Three Methods of Teaching Social Studies Concepts to Fourth-Grade Students: An Aptitude-Treatment Interaction Study," *American Educational Research Journal*, 20, 1983-663-670.

Massialas, B., and B. Cox, *Inquiry in Social Studies*. New York: McGraw-Hill, 1966.

Mueller, Daniel J., "Mastery Learning: Partly Boon, Partly Boondoggle," *Teacher's College Record*, 78, Sept. 1976, 41-52.

McDaid, Janet L., and Donna G. Davis, "Using Assessment
    Results Wisely (For Improving Curriculum and Instructional
    Strategies)," *Thrust for Educational Leadership*, 21, 1991, 34-6.
National Council for the Social Studies (Lawrence Metcalf, ed.). 1971.
Nesbitt, W.A., *Simulation Games for the Social Studies
    Classroom*. New York: Foreign Policy Association, 1971.
Oliver, D.W., and J.P. Shaver, "The Effect of Student
    Characteristics and Teaching Method Interactions on Learning to
    Think Critically." Paper presented to the American Educational
    Research Association, 1968.
Oxford, Rebecca L, and David Crookall, "Research on Language
    Learning Strategies: Methods, Findings, and Instructional
    Issues," *The Modern Language Journal*, 73, 1989, 404-19.
Parker, Jeanette Plauch, "Instructional Strategies for Teaching the
    Gifted," *The Gifted Child Today*, 14, 1991, 28.
Peat, D., R.F. Mulcahy, and J. Darko-Yeboah, "SPELT
    (Strategies Program for Effective Learning/Thinking): a
    description and analysis of instructional procedures," *Instructional
    Science*, 18, 1989, 95-118.
Ricca, Judith, "Learning Styles and Preferred Instructional
    Strategies of Gifted Students," *Gifted Child Quarterly*, 28, 1984,
    121-6.
Rist, Ray C., "Student Social Class and Teacher Expectations: The
    Self-Fulfilling Prophecy in Ghetto Education," *Harvard
    Educational Review*, 40, August, 1970, 411-451.
Rist, Ray C., "Social Distance and Social Inequality in a Ghetto
    Kindergarten Classroom," *Urban Education*, 7, October,1972,
    241-260.
Rodriguez, Stephen, Robert E. Stephens, and Sarah Arena,
    "Interviewing Subject-matter Experts: Strategies for Instructional
    Design Success," *Educational Technology*, 31, 1991, 27-32.
Shaftel, F., and G. Shaftel, *Role Playing for Social Values
    Decision Making in the Social Studies*. Englewood Cliffs, N.J.:
    Prentice-Hall, 1982
Shaftel, Fannie, and George Shaftel, *Role Playing in the
    Curriculum*. Englewood Cliffs, N.J.: Prentice-Hall, 1982.

Sharan, S., and Y. Sharan, *Small-Group Teaching*. Englewood Cliffs, J.J.: Educational Technology Publications, 1976.Sharan, S., "Cooperative Learning in Small Groups: Recent Methods and Effects on Achievement, Attitudes, and Ethnic Relations," *Review of Educational Research*, 50, 1980, 241-71.

Shaver, James P., and William Strong, *Facing Value-Decisions: Rationale-Building for Teachers*. New York: Teachers College Press, 1982.

Sigel, I.E., and F.H. Hooper, *Logical Thinking in Children*. New York: Holt, Rinehart, & Winston, 1968.

Simon, S. & Clark, J., *Beginning Values Clarification*. New York: Pennant Press, 1975.

Skinner, B.F., *The Technology of Teaching*. Englewood Cliffs, N.J.: Prentice-Hall, Inc., 1968.

Slavin, R., *Cooperative Learning*. New York: Longman, 1983.

Suchman, J., "Studies in Inquiry Training," in *Piaget Reconsidered*, eds. R. Ripple and V. Bookcastle. Ithaca, N.Y.: Cornell University, 1964.

"Symposium: Cognitive-developmental Issues and Instructional Strategies," *Contemporary Educational Psychology*, 13, 1988, 185-307.

Taber, J., R. Glaser, and H.S. Halmuth, *Learning and Programmed Instruction*. Reading, Mass: Addison-Wesley Publishing company, Inc., 1967.

Taylor, C., ed. *Creativity: Progress and Potential*. New York: McGraw-Hill, 1964

Tennyson, Robert D., Robert L. Elmore, and Leonard Snyder, "Advancements in Instructional Design Theory: Contextual Module analysis and Integrated Instructional Strategies," *Educ. Technology Research & Development*, 40,1992, 9-22.

Thelen, H., *Classroom Grouping for Teachability*. New York: John Wiley & Sons, Inc., 1967.

Torrance, E.P., *Guiding Creative Talent*. Englewood Cliffs, N.J.: Prentice-Hall, Inc., 1962.

Unruh, Roy D., Lyn Le Countryman, and Timothy M. Cooney, "The PRISMS Approach (Physics Resource and Instructional

Strategies for Motivating Students)," *The Science Teacher*, 59, 1992, 36-41.

Van Patten, James, Chun-I Chao, and Charles M. Reigeluth, "A Review of Strategies for Sequencing and Synthesizing Instruction," *Review of Educational Research*, 56, 1986, 437-71.

Von Haden, Herbert I. & Jean M. King, *Innovations in Education: Their Pro's and Con's*, Worthington,OH: Chas. Jones Pub. Co., 1971.

Weimer, Maryellen, "Improving College Teaching; Strategies for Developing Instructional Effectiveness," *Teaching Sociology*, 19, 1991, 287-8.

Weimer, Maryellen, "Improving College Teaching; Strategies for Developing Instructional Effectiveness," *The Journal of Higher Education*, 62, 1991, 237-9.

Weston, Cynthia, and Patricia A. Cranton, "Selecting Instructional Strategies," *The Journal of Higher Education* 57, 1986, 259-88.

Willis, Barry, "Instructional Development in Higher Education: Strategies that Work," *Educational Technology*, 24, 1984, 31-2.

Wilson, John E., and Claire E. Weinstein, "Identifying and Evaluating Potential Instructional Components for High School Learning Strategies Programs," *The High School Journal*, 72, 1989, 136-42.

ORDER FORM

Please send me _____ copies of *THE EXPERT EDUCATOR*
A Reference Manual of Teaching Strategies for Quality
Education...by Anthony S. Dallmann-Jones, Ph.D.

To:

Name _____

Address_____

City _____ State _____ Zip _____

Shipping---Book rate: $3.00 for 1st and $1.00 for each additional
          Enclose Check or Money Order for
          $29.95 per book + shipping = $ _____
          (Wisc. residents add 5% tax)   (amt. enclosed)
          (Please Allow 2-3 weeks for delivery)

Mail to: Three Blue Herons Publishing, Inc., P.O. Box 463,
          Fond du Lac, WI 54936-0463

(To make *The Expert Educator* part of your media center's
professional reference library we have added a convenience form)

To: MEDIA CENTER or _____ Date:_____

From: _____Dept:_____

MEDIA CENTER ORDER FORM

Please send _____copies of *THE EXPERT EDUCATOR*
A Reference Manual of Teaching Strategies...
by Anthony S. Dallmann-Jones, Ph.D.   ISBN# 1-881952-23-1

Shipping---Book rate: $3.00 for 1st and $1.00 for each additional
          Enclose Check, M.O. or P.O. # _____
          $29.95 per book + shipping = $ _____
          (Wisc. residents add 5% tax)   (amt. enclosed)
          (Please Allow 2-3 weeks for delivery)

Purchase from: **THREE BLUE HERONS PUBLISHING INC.**
P.O. Box 463, Fond du Lac, WI 54936-0463   Ph. (414) 921-6991

ORDER FORM

Other products from THREE BLUE HERONS PUBLISHING, INC.
featuring
Anthony S. Dallmann-Jones, Ph.D.

VIDEOTAPES

Dysfunctional Family Survivor Dynamics In The Classroom (75 minutes; color; copyright 1993) An interview in which Dr. Dallmann-Jones thoroughly describes the manner in which children's family of origin issues impact the school environment. Explains why so many of the critical issues in education are misdiagnosed and provides effective solutions for teachers. Should be in every school's professional library! ($49.95 + $3.00 shipping)   Send me:___x $52.95 =_____

Self-Esteem for Survivors of Dysfunctional Families (70 minutes; color; copyright 1993) Dr. Dallmann-Jones offers an innovative approach with a practical program for discovering students' healthy self-esteem-- a must if dysfunctional family survivors are to break the cycle of abuse and self-neglect. An important film for any educator who works with children coming to school from non-nurturing homes. Very powerful. ($49.95 + $3.00 shipping) Send me:___x $52.95 =_____

AUDIOTAPE

Stress Management & Relaxation (90 minutes, copyright 1993) A progressive 5-Element guided meditation by Dr. Dallmann-Jones taped at Calfrin Waterfall. Flip side is 45 minutes of ocean and surf sounds as a backdrop for practicing the 5 elements or just for soothing relaxation. ($10.00 + $2.00 shipping) Send me:____ x $12 =_____

(Wisc. residents add 5% to total)   **TOTAL:**_____

Send Check, money order or purchase order #_____
to: **Three Blue Herons Publishing, Inc. PO Box 463**
          Fond du Lac, WI 54935-0463 Ph.(414-921-6991)
Ship to:
NAME_____
STREET_____
CITY_____STATE_____ZIP_____

(Please allow 2-3 weeks for delivery)

ABOUT THE AUTHORS

Anthony S. Dallmann-Jones, Ph.D. is a graduate professor of educational psychology at Marian College in Fond du Lac, Wisconsin. He is Director of the Institute of Transformational Studies, a consulting firm that designs and produces vehicles, bridges and scaffolding for positive human and organizational transformation. He has authored many books, monographs, articles, and tapes and conducted numerous trainings and seminars across the United States and Canada.

The Black River Group is a national educational think tank based in Sheboygan, Wisconsin. A team of five educators with over 150 years of experience and expertise in every facet of education, BRG is dedicated to working closely with schools and organizations as a catalyst to facilitate the development of proactive and successful learning environments. BRG members have worked with some of the most difficult problems facing schools and their communities and are known for their "1000 Day Commitment Plan."

Members of **The Black River Group**:

Claudia Bricks, M.S.   Patrick Mealy, M.S.
Rick Osterhaus, M.S.   Steve Smith, Ed.D.
Anthony S. Dallmann-Jones, Ph.D.

314 Pioneer Road Sheboygan, WI 53081   (414) 457-0525

"Support the best and transform the rest."